AUTISM?
ASPERGERS?
ADHD? ADD?

A Parent's Roadmap
to Understanding and Support!

Diane Drake Burns

AUTISM? ASPERGERS? ADHD? ADD?
A Parent's Roadmap to Understanding and Support

All marketing and publishing rights guaranteed to and reserved by

FUTURE HORIZONS INC.

721 W. Abram Street
Arlington, Texas 76013
800-489-0727
817-277-0727
817-277-2270 (fax)
E-mail: info@futurehorizons-autism.com
www.FutureHorizons-autism.com

Cover design and book layout: Matt Mitchell, www.mattmitchelldesign.com

Printed in the United States of America.

ISBN 1-932565-26-4

TABLE OF CONTENTS

PROLOGUE

Abbott and Costello, the great comedy duo of the late thirties, are remembered for a particularly mind-numbing skit called, "Who's on First?" The baseball scenario involves players with names like Who, What and I Don't Know. Who is on first, What is on second and I Don't Know is on third. You can imagine the confusion as the comedy team juggles the mix of names.

Here's a variation of that entertaining skit and while it's just as confusing, it's not quite so funny.

Parent: I see Normal's playing first today.

Coach: Nope, that's ADD.

Parent: But he looks so much like Normal.

Coach: I know what you mean. But he was definitely ADD when I did the roster.

Parent: Then, is that Normal on second?

Coach: Nope, that's ADHD, although sometimes he's only ADD.

Parent: Okay, but I'm sure that's Normal playing third. He's so good at this game.

Coach: Wrong again, that's Aspergers. He was playing ADD, but now that he's older, we've decided he was Aspergers the whole time.

Parent: Then that must be Normal at bat. He really looks good.

Coach: Nope, that's Autism, but I've just about decided he's a better Aspergers. Sometimes even I can't tell the difference.

Parent: So where is Normal?

Coach: To be honest, I'm not sure he's on our team.

Autism? Asperger's Syndrome? ADHD? ADD? Can we all agree that figuring out the elusive label, whether it's your first child in diapers or your fifth in high school, isn't easy? Even the doctors aren't quite sure what to make of it.

So how does a parent decide if a child is normal, pin the right label on them, and then figure out how to help?

The only way to start is by getting into the game. Your job, the most important job, the why-you-are-reading-this-book job, is to make the subject of your child's differences a priority. No more waiting until they're older or wishing they'd grow out of it.

This little book will ease you out of the stands and onto the field, to join the crowd of parents already on their way to understanding their child's unique shade of normal. You'll find your position, learn the rules, and promise to play until the game is won.

CHAPTER ONE

Was That The Exit to Normal?

With three kids between the ages of four and twelve, I get to experience the best movies Hollywood has to offer. One of my favorites is *The Emperor's New Groove.*

Early in the story, Emperor Cusco has been turned into a llama. He and his human traveling companion Pacha are trapped, inescapably bound to opposite sides of a log as it floats upright down a rushing river. Pacha is the first to hint at what's ahead.

> "Uh-oh," says Pacha, facing downstream.
>
> "Don't tell me," deadpans the emperor-turned-llama, "we're about to go over a huge waterfall."
>
> "Yep," Pacha drawls from the other side of the log.
>
> "Sharp rocks at the bottom?"
>
> "Most likely," Pacha answers in a carefree sort of way.

There is a dramatic pause when Cusco, staring into the camera with a deadly gleam in his eye, says, "Bring it on."

Emperor Cusco and Pacha plunge over the waterfall, screaming maniacally, only to survive their near-death experience with Disney-like magic.

WELCOME TO OUR WORLD

Wouldn't it be great if we felt like that in real life? Got troubles? Bring it on. Feeling a little overwhelmed today? Bring it on, baby!

But that's not anybody's reality. For most of us, real life includes waterfalls of fear and failure as we work to provide for our families and try to be good parents. Painful circumstances often sabotage our hopes and dreams. Yet there's enough blessings and beauty in each day to recover from the struggles, to help us get ready to live another day.

Then there are those families, like yours maybe, who are special enough to have been given the gift of a *different* child. For you, the stress and strain of trying to do the right thing goes way beyond the ups and downs of real life. You really are plunging headfirst over a waterfall, and without one speck of Disney's animated power.

WAS THAT THE EXIT TO NORMAL?

Hollywood knows all about great story lines and happy endings. Dorothy arrives safely back in Kansas, Woody makes it back to Andy in *Toy Story*, and ET comes back to life just in time to board the "Mothership".

Families with a different child are trying to get home too, in a way, to that elusive place called "Normal".

MY LIFE: THE MOVIE

My own family's journey went something like this:

My husband Bill and I embarked enthusiastically on our road trip through life as responsible parents, reasonably in control. He drove while I read the map. But as Jonathan, our second child, approached the two-year mile-marker, we both sensed something was wrong.

"Is this kid normal?" we mumbled secretively to each other. In my road-trip analogy, what we were really saying went something like, "Is that a bridge out up ahead?"

I reacted to the confusion like any normal parent. I flung myself across the emergency brake, (which, of course, didn't work because families don't ever get to stop), overcorrected the steering wheel, and then jumped up to analyze the situation, only to realize I had no facts.

"There can't be a bridge out up ahead," I yelled to Bill, "That's not what's on the map!" Friends in their snazzy, sleek cars drove effortlessly past us, while our own efforts resembled Lucille Ball in a Winnebago.

No big deal, I consoled myself, we're not far enough along on our journey, anyway. Surely our family will get to Normal soon. I was determined not to worry.

But I did worry.

Bill and I realized our carefully planned road trip of raising a family had become something quite different—as we watched our son grow more different every day. And then came the moment we had to admit to ourselves that something was wrong; that we'd lost our way.

"Hmmm," I said to Bill as we sped along our way, "could that have been..." and with numbing reality, we turned to watch the last possible exit to Normal fade from view.

I KNOW MY CHILD IS DIFFERENT

Good news. Those days of maniacal driving are long past. Like Emperor Cusco, I eventually found my own determined gleam and confident voice to tell the doctor or teacher, even God, to "bring it on". My only regret is that it took me such a long time to recognize that I needed a map—a *different* map because I had a *different* child.

I often wonder what would have happened if someone had stopped me along the way and said, "I see your child is different, can I tell you what to do?"

Are you wondering if you missed that exit to Normal, or, Heaven help us, you know you missed it but haven't the slightest idea how to get back?

Is the trip thing going okay but you've felt the doubts disguised by shadowed remarks like, "Your child is just a little different. I'm sure he'll be okay."

Do you have a child who doesn't quite fit your definition of 'normal'?

Please read on.

NORMAL WHO?

I've decided "normal" is an alien word. My own definition would read something like this: the opposite of different, totally subjective, having at least a million meanings—you pick. My four-year-old daughter knows what a *cyborg* is and wants her own mechanical arm while my twelve-year-old son wouldn't know a clean pair of underwear if it jumped up and bit him on the you-know-what.

Are they normal? Of course they are. A parent knows, or *feels*, from the first child on, when that broad definition of normal fits and when it doesn't.

For several years, those wild years in the Winnebago, I analyzed, I pondered, I denied—all over the question of normal. I shared my doubts but buried my fears. I was waiting for something, I just didn't know what. *Can't I stay confused and things still turn out okay?*

IT WON'T GO AWAY

I once knew an intelligent young woman, early twenties, college grad, who was in a horrible skiing accident. It was at a company retreat in Colorado, and on her way down the mountain to watch the Dallas Cowboys play, she hit a tree. She had been contemplating her beautiful form, the way her feet were so close together, skis parallel. But suddenly there was that tree, and in a fraction of a second, she was wrapped around it the wrong way. It really hurt. At least, that's what she told me.

The young woman was rescued, x-rayed, and then driven to the nearest hospital. More x-rays showed a fracture in one of the lower vertebrae. Serious, yes; but she was told the paralysis would soon go away. The hospital sent her home with simple parting instructions. "See a doctor immediately!"

Miss Responsible went back to her Texas home but never saw a doctor. She never asked for help. She grinned and bore the pain for about six months, walking with a dramatic limp for even longer.

Why? Because she feared the unknown, words that might expect some action she couldn't handle. She feared the unpredictable challenges, the expense. She stayed in her safe though painful world and chose to ignore the little voice inside her saying, get help. She figured if she could stand the pain, it would eventually go away.

Now, over twenty years later, she still experiences the consequences of that "independent" approach.

It's hard to believe people like that exist, but we do.

DETERMINED DUMMY

I was determined to drag my feet into the world of developmental differences. For three years, I careened down that road in my Winnebago, obviously nowhere near Normal.

I routinely picked up the obligatory book on the subject, but after reading the first chapter, I would slam the cover shut and drop it in the nearest wastebasket. Their stories made me cry. They were depressing. And, I reasoned with myself, Jonathan was certainly not as bad off as the children in those books.

Besides, how could I judge what others had to say when I could hardly put my own questions into words? All I was sure about was that in seemingly small ways, my child was different. And just like my skiing accident, I was afraid to do something about it.

THE ARGUMENTS

Maybe you don't know *what* or *if* you need help. Who gave you this book anyway? Why keep reading when there are sure to be unattractive possibilities that might only make you feel bad? Why read this book?

For your child.

My family suffered for my delay and I sincerely regret that the person it hurt the most was my son. That's what gives me the passion to ask you to look for answers when you hardly know the questions.

Please read on.

COME WITH ME

I believe there's a reason you're holding this little book in your hand:

- ☒ Because you have a baby, a toddler, a teen, who's in some way, "different".

- ☒ Because I will never assume what applies to you or what your child's needs are.

☒ Because I believe there is a direct correlation between beginning treatment and degree of recovery. Whether you are sure or not of your child's issues, protect your chances to help your child (ages eighteen months to five years is the ideal). It is also never too late!

☒ Because I want to satisfy your curiosities, address questions you may have had about your child, or pass along an explanation about the differences you're observing.

☒ Because you want to avoid drugs if possible, or you're tired of trying to figure out the right drug cocktail and wonder if there's something else you could be doing.

☒ Because I want you to feel comfortable enough to read the words that are simply possibilities, commonalities, and options. I want you to be courageous enough to peer a little further up the road and not wait, like I did, for a crisis.

☒ Because I'd like to give you encouragement and hope. I'd like to put my hand gently at your back and steer you forward, instead of seeing you hang back, ignoring things, toughing it out; all at the risk of watching you struggle to regain your joy.

☒ Because I don't want you to miss one more day of helping your child.

LITTLE BITES

This handbook is a covered bridge to help you face the sinking feeling that maybe you've missed your exit to Normal. It's like mild salsa, because that's all you need. No dramatics, no doomsday predictions and certainly no emphatic declarations of a diagnosis. It's just a handbook about what to do if your child is different.

This handbook is fear-proof. The chapters come in very small bites. You read one, chew on it a while, keep chewing on it until you're completely sure you're done with it, then maybe, if the sky is blue and you didn't gain any weight even though you had ice cream every night this week, you go on to the next chapter.

You might not pick the book back up for weeks. But when you do, it will be there to answer one more question. I hope you'll pick it up when you need to feel better.

A PROMISE

One last promise: I'm saving my story for the very last chapter, right before all those resources that are a lot smarter than I am. We all have a story, but since I can't hear yours, I think it's only fair to make mine optional. You read it if and when you want to, but on one condition. That you don't read the last chapter first and THEN throw the book away.

CHAPTER TWO

Rules of the Road

ADVICE? FORGET IT

Five years ago, I came out of the closet and declared myself a writer. I'd written no more than a lot of people, but there was this new empowerment that came over me when faced with that oft-put question, "What do you do?"

Saying, "I'm a writer," made me smile every time.

Within two days of my self-declaration, I was on my way home from a late-night meeting when I heard a well-respected author being interviewed on a talk show.

"Tell me, Mr. Jenkins," began the talk show host, "if there was someone out there listening right now, *right now,* who wanted to be a writer but didn't know how to get started, what would you tell them?"

I pulled over into a parking lot and literally stared at the radio, holding my breath, waiting for this man whom I admired and respected to talk to *me.*

"The most important thing I'd tell them is don't even think about beginning their writing career with a novel. It's like going to graduate school before you've been to grade school. It's a very difficult, frustrating process for even the seasoned writer. I would definitely tell a new writer to do *anything* other than start with a novel."

I was so inspired, I rushed home and began my first novel.

MY KIND OF ADVICE

If only Mr. Jenkins had said, "I suggest you start with a smaller project, **but**, if you must write a novel, take a class, read a book, and know that it will probably take you twice as long to write it." I wish I'd had some advice to go along with doing things my way, the hard way. It would have made the rough road I chose a little bit easier.

No matter what I say about how to help a different child, you will, no doubt, do it your way. I also know that whatever you choose to do won't be easy. It's all difficult. That's why, along with plenty of finger-wagging facts, I've tried to include real-life advice to show you what happens regardless of whose advice you've taken. I hope when you hit the rough spots, you'll be prepared. Here are a few hard-learned lessons I'd like to pass on.

Listen

Learn how to listen. When a toddler asks, "Where do babies come from?", only a word or two is necessary to satisfy his curiosity. But let a parent of a different child raise her hand to ask a question, and watch out! She's likely to get a dissertation.

Don't let that stop you from listening. This isn't a "my way or the highway" road trip. Every child is different and experiences are abundant, so you have to listen to a lot of ideas to find what's right for you.

Remember, you don't need to try every suggestion. At the same time, don't let the ramblings of a passionate mother make you want to ignore the alternate routes.

Be ready for that urge to put up walls, to shut out well-meaning individuals, until you can't hear what they're saying.

You don't have to take any route. You can always turn back and you most certainly can pull off to rethink what to do.

Personally, 90 percent of the gold, the stuff that helped Jonathan the most, came from other mothers. I hate to think of where we'd be if I hadn't been listening.

Pace Yourself

Learn to listen to yourself. Don't push too hard up 'Learning Curve' mountain. I learned my lesson after a late-night phone call from a mother in Wichita Falls, Texas. Referred by my pediatrician, she wanted to know what I'd done with Jonathan and, because we'd seen such success, I assumed she wanted to know everything. I made the mistake of telling her everything. We were on the phone for over three hours that night and neither the pediatrician nor I have heard from her since. I'm sure the poor woman is still buried under the mental to-do list I gave her.

In my excitement to help, I'd forgotten how steep the learning curve can be. I wish she'd told me, rather begged me, to stop.

If someone's "help" is overwhelming, don't hesitate to say, "Enough!" Do what you can, as you can.

Peaks and Valleys

Look for the peaks and valleys. These are the highs and lows of taking in new information and tackling a new course of action. Some months I made calls, dealt with insurance, read books, etc. Some months I ignored information completely.

If, at times, you're feeling overwhelmed, don't add anything to your plate. Wait until you're hungry again.

Traveling Companions

Find yourself a driving buddy. Someone you can be starkly honest with, who empathizes with you because they either experience the same struggles or they just happen to be incredibly kind. Your struggles are meant to be shared.

I tried driving alone for about four years. I thought I was being open with the people around me, my friends, our church family, etc. But really, I wasn't. At the end of that time period, I was lower than low. I realized there was still a part of me hiding. Do you know how much energy it takes to hide? When I finally blurted out to a group of friends what I was going through, the outpouring of love and support was tremendous.

Determine to begin talking about your concerns. Look for situations where you can drop a hint about what you're going through. Because you need others, force yourself to follow up with suggested help (names or numbers). Check out the web sites listed in the Resources section at the end of the book. It's full of parents *just like you*. Eventually, you'll find a soul mate who will understand you like no other.

If you're lucky, you'll find a friend like I did. Jennifer was a classic type-A personality. She read everything, did research to the ninth degree, and surfed the Internet daily, constantly communicating with other moms and doctors. My job was to call her up and take notes.

See, it's even okay to be lazy. The point is that a driving buddy will shorten the trip. They'll even remind you to laugh.

Travel Light

Throw out any excess baggage. Having a *different* child is a JOB, and the lighter your load, the better. You can't be room mom, den mother, garden club program chair, Sunday School teacher and learn about that road that might not take you to Normal.

You can always hang out a sign later that says *Volunteer Available Here*. It won't take long to fill your calendar.

YOU'RE DOING GREAT

Remember, take baby steps. Let yourself go at your own pace. Read one chapter, then, if you need to, close the book. It will keep. If you barrel through in one sitting, you'll throw it away. And then you won't be able to help anyone.

CHAPTER THREE

Questions Are The Key

QUESTIONS SCARE ME

I admit I've never been good at asking questions. They scare me. They scare me because the really important ones sound so much like confrontation. Questions like, "Is this the right classroom situation for my child?" and, "Do you know where that little bruise on his arm came from?" don't sound very nice. They infer things like, "I don't trust your judgment," and, "What exactly are your motives regarding my child?"

On the rare occasion I do drum up enough courage to ask a tough question, my hearty conscience yells something helpful like, "And who do you think you are?!"

That's when I remind myself of an important piece of advice, the gift of a very wise mother. She said, "If you don't fight for your child, no one else will."

The different child is depending on you to find a way, get help, to accept no less than the best. Fighting means listening better, observing more, and reading more. It especially means asking the tough questions.

I think the road back to Normal begins with questions. So, from an admitted chicken, let me lead you toward the light. Together, we're going to ask some tough questions.

MOTHER KNOWS BEST

Differences in Jonathan began to surface when he was about eighteen months old. Nothing bad, more like a 'lack of change' than anything else. For the next year and a half, I kept worry to a minimum, passively wondering whether or not my child was normal. (As I've admitted earlier, I have this uncanny ability to ignore the uncomfortable.) I do take credit for one decisive move. "When he's three, and *if* there are still issues, *then* I'll get some help."

Of course, Jonathan turned three and there were clear differences. I reluctantly made the phone call to set up an appointment with a developmental pediatrician.

Arriving home later that day, I recounted to my mother all the doctor had said. Casually, she asked, "Do you think Jonathan might have..." and then she said the "A" word.

"Jonathan is normal in almost every way," I stammered. Hadn't I just told her the doctor preceded almost every sentence with maybe? "Maybe he's got this, maybe he's got that...." How dare someone suggest my beautiful little boy had some ugly sounding 'thing'? I silenced her with a look and time marched on.

I realize now that the pediatrician was being gentle and my mother, honest. I was blatantly terrified.

UNSPOKEN REALITIES

The truth is, the only thing scarier than our questions are those unspoken realities. Don't do as I did and avoid the questions. It's time to be as honest as possible about where your child is and to put those thoughts into words. I know it's hard, but this is a safe place.

If you'll talk with me here, it will be easier to talk about it out there.

Back to the Winnebago. Remember what it's like to wish you had a better road map? What would you say if I told you the map is there, and you just don't know how to read it?

It all starts with questions.

NO WRONG ANSWERS

Let's begin with me asking you a few basic questions and please relax, there are no wrong answers.

- ☒ Is it a struggle to explain your doubts or fears about your child to friends and family?

- ☒ Do you feel inadequate trying to explain your child's needs to childcare workers, the church nursery, or to a baby-sitter?

- ☒ At checkup time, do you arrive at the doctor's with questions in hand, then hesitate to say anything; or, the doctor offers you a simple explanation and yet, at home, the questions seem unanswered?

☒ Do you feel the need to explain your child to others?

☒ Do you need help?

If you answered "yes" even reluctantly, you're on the right track to being the greatest advocate your child has ever had.

If, by the way, you answered "yes" loudly, impatiently, then the rest will be a breeze.

ASK YOURSELF:

Questions lead to understanding your child. It's time to come up with your own. Here are some ideas to get you started.

1. Why doesn't Zoe play like other children?

2. Why does she find a specific toy so fascinating? She can play with it for hours and then screams, terrified, when I take it away?

3. Why does she have trouble in the car when I turn on the radio or change the channel?

4. Why can't Zoe sit still or why does she crawl under a chair when everyone else is sitting?

5. Why do certain seemingly insignificant things make her cry, like wearing socks or the sound of rain?

6. Why does it take her such a long time to recover from a stressful experience, like leaving the park or pool or when I deny her a treat?

7. Why is conversation not normal (too much, too little, 'her' world, disconnected...)?

8. Why do I have to repeat myself five times to be heard?

Start with the basic reality that your child is different. Now's the time to begin articulating the ways in which she is different. Go through your week with a pencil and paper close at hand. **The more questions you come up with, the more answers you will find.**

Before you start, though, I have another bag of tricks. It's not chocolate but it might help.

You're Not Alone

This is hard. Incredibly hard. For me, every time a new question (those nagging realities of things that weren't normal) formed in my mind, I had to start crying all over again.

"He's never going to talk," *boo hoo*, "he's never going to poop in the potty," *woe is me*, "he hates me" *sob sob*.

Sometimes it helps just knowing you're not alone. I feel for you and the hard times to come. But I made it and you will too.

Remember, I was a lousy Winnebago driver trying to keep a dozen plates spinning in the air. You're going to be the "bring it on" mamma, able to handle every question your brain can throw at you.

Stay in the Present

Trying to explain a child is scary. While reluctantly searching for answers, I felt like I was stumbling through a haunted house, forced to reach into some deep, dark pit for answers that had their own horrible endings.

Don't let yourself get too carried away with, *What am I going to do with what I find out?* Try to stay in the present, not the future.

Take off the Mommy Hat

You are now a scientist, an annoying statistician and that makes precious Zoe or Clarence a cute little lab rat.

As you're learning the system surrounding developmental differences, it's helpful to see it like a JOB. Observe. Take notes. Research. Compare your notes with others.

This is the most difficult job in the world. It's all the hard parts of being a mother put together *to the hundredth power,* though at times it can be very interesting and rewarding. But even when it's not, you do it. Trust me, it will all be worth it.

> **Warning:** Watch for signs that you've put the Mommy hat back on. You'll feel sorry for your child, for yourself, your family, the whole world! Don't leave that hat on too long.

Do Your Digging in Times of Strength

Do your digging in times of strength or you'll lose your drive. When you're on that mountainous learning curve, listen to yourself; valid feelings of being overwhelmed, fear and exhaustion should tell you to stop climbing, but only until you're ready to start again.

Have an Escape

I obviously love movies. I do my best thinking after two hours of mindless entertainment. I forget the latest conflict at home and laugh out loud at other's misfortunes. I can think. Most importantly, I can listen to my soul.

If you can't get away, I hope you have an escape pod. A wise woman once said, "Give a woman her own room and she can do anything". Few of us have a whole room but there has to be a spot where you feel safe. Even if it's in the middle of the room, it has your chair, your pillow, or it's next to a window. Closets and bathrooms work, too, but I hope someone gives you an upgrade.

Hold on to Hope

There are so many reasons for asking tough questions, but I think the most significant one is hope. Every question, every answer, lays a foundation of understanding and direction on which to build our hope, of helping a child. But that requires putting pen to paper, putting something into words.

Asking questions is also the beginning of your story, eventually becoming hope for others.

Tools with a Purpose

The questions are essential. I often have to remind my kids that something is either a *tool* or a *toy*. Questions are the tools you need to lead you to answers.

Don't Forget the Perks

Believe it or not, someday, all the talking about questions and future and struggles, will come easily. You'll be "that really smart mother" with all the answers at your fingertips. You'll have a whole new vocabulary. The inexperienced will think you're brilliant and start referring to you in angelic terms. You'll be spouting statistics and chemical compounds to complete strangers if you think it will help. You'll help carry the load for another struggling parent.

Accept the Growing Pains

As a child, I experienced the misery of growing pains. My muscles and joints ached so badly, all I could do was curl up in a ball on the bed with my heating pad and cry.

I didn't even grow that much. But now I understand how it feels when my own kids start groaning with an aching joint. First, I give them some Tylenol. Then, I rub their legs and tell them what's happening, at least what I imagine to be happening.

I explain that their muscles and bones are growing. I tell them I know just how it hurts. Then I tell them I know it's only for a little while. And someday, they'll be tall and grown-up. It will all be worth it.

That's what you're going through. It hurts to have to grow. We stare new information or experience in the face, stamp our feet and say, "I don't want to learn about this! This is not what I planned to do with my life!"

Do that if you have to. Lock yourself in a bathroom, scream out loud, and then take a few deep breaths. Remind yourself that there is hope. God determined it was best to put this child in your care, whatever capacity that may be. Don't give up. Don't lose your hope. Take one step at a time.

Now stand up straight, look your tear-stained face straight in the eye, and tell yourself it's going to be okay. You have to grow up in a whole new realm and it's not going to last forever. Someday, you'll be tall and grown-up and it will all be worth it.

> *For me, asking questions means understanding my son, and in the end, loving him more like God intends. When I wonder at night what God's purpose might be for Jonathan, I usually come to this conclusion: God is using Jonathan to change me, for the good of His plan.*

DONE, TIME TO...

Now that I've told you to be brave and determined, I have to admit it's mostly talk. It still hurts, it's still hard and it's still a process, a go-at-your-own-pace course.

Write down your questions, and then test yourself before going on to the next chapter. As you read over your list, do you start to cry? Be honest. A few tears are normal, but if you start to sob, take a break. Don't go on to the next chapter. Wait until you can read your list with a little bit of distance, a "Hey, these are a few things I've been wondering about" kind of attitude.

Don't be deceived by well-meaning friends. If they get hold of your questions and say something like, "Oh, I don't think little Clarence does that," or, "Remember, Einstein didn't speak (or read or burp or *something*) until he was five," grab the list out of their hands and say thank you very much.

Now, write down your questions. Don't go on to the next chapter until you're ready.

_____

_____

_____

_____

_____

_____

_____

_____

_____

_____

_____

_____

_____

_____

A COFFEE BREAK
BETWEEN CHAPTERS

Now that you've got your list of questions, you've got to find the answers. Let's see, that shouldn't be too hard. There's only the school system, private specialists, therapists, doctors, referrals, the expensive ones, the freebies, and the books to choose from! This is the moment you feel like you're standing in front of the Rocky Mountains for the first time and someone says, "Go on now, just get across the best way you can."

I know exactly how you feel. Is it possible to figure it out? Where do you start? Will you ever survive? The answers are: Yes, I'll tell you, and yes.

But first, let's take a quick coffee break.

Those two characters in *Emperor's New Groove* floating up and over a waterfall is a pretty funny scene. But here's an even better one. In the movie *Bowfinger*, Steve Martin plays a down-and-out movie producer who's determined to make an action movie with the most famous actor of the day, Kit Ramsey, played by Eddie Murphy. The only problem is, Kit isn't interested in making a movie with Mr. Bowfinger.

Ironically, Kit has a twin brother, Jiff, also played by Murphy. Jiff, rather than being muscular and cool like his brother, is repulsive, all the way down to the generous bits of spittle dangling from his steely braces.

In this memorable scene, the movie crew is setting up Jiff's big shot along the L.A. Freeway. Bowfinger explains to the buffoonish Jiff that the scene calls for him to *dash* across eight lanes of traffic and into the arms of his awaiting love. In the seconds it takes for Steve Martin to explain this to Eddie Murphy, what seems like hundreds, perhaps thousands of cars have jetted across the screen. The noise is deafening and you can almost feel the heat off the concrete. We all know it's a death sentence, except for idiot Jiff.

It's hard to tell if Jiff is squinting or smiling as he listens to his instructions, and only once does he look at the freeway, inches away and says, "Gee, aren't they going kinda fast?"

"Oh, don't worry about that," Bowfinger says, "they're all stunt drivers," which we know, of course, they're not.

Next, we see Eddie Murphy on the other side of the freeway, plastered to the concrete wall, braces glinting in the sun, as cars race past, virtually inches from his face. Martin, standing with the movie crew, eight lanes away, yells, "Action!"

Choking with laughter, we watch Jiff dart across the L.A. expressway. By the time he gets to the director, he can hardly talk, he's so traumatized. The director then makes him do it one more time, just to be sure they have the shot. By this time, Jiff is hysterical. "*Please*, Mr. Bowfinger," he begs, "can't I go get coffee for the guys? I don't want to be an actor anymore, I just want to go to Starbucks and get coffee for the crew." Only in the movies.

I thought this might be a good time to remind ourselves that after a good dose of stress, we all need a break. Stress makes you want to quit. It burns little holes in your brain, allows bothersome viruses to pop up as cold sores, gives you migraines, a touch of depression or just makes you feel crummy.

If you've been at this awhile, give yourself a break. Get a magazine and just look at the pictures and forget for a day that everything in your life is urgent. Take a break from this book if you need to. But don't take too long. If your child is different….

The next chapter talks to the parent who acknowledges that their child is different and that there's something to be done now. It's for the parent who says, "I realize my child, rather than becoming more normal every day, is not, which means they are becoming more different. I don't want that and I need to do something now."

CHAPTER FOUR

Finding Answers

THE WIDE, WIDE WORLD OF POSSIBILITY

Welcome to the world of possibilities! Give yourself a pat on the back for making it this far. By turning the page, you've proven to yourself that you want to dig deeper into why your child is different. Armed with a tangible list of questions, you want answers. And whether or not you feel ready to take the next step, trust me, you are.

I WANT ANSWERS!

I felt like a mother about to give birth as Jonathan and I followed our map to the largest, most prestigious children's medical center in Dallas. "Pediatric Neurologist" sounded so fascinating, so brilliant! *Finally*, I thought, *a doctor who will shine his little pen light into the darkest regions of Jonathan's brain. Finally, someone to tell me exactly what is wrong and then exactly what to do!* I could hardly wait.

Our pediatrician had made the appointment and on that bright sunny morning in April, 1997, my four-year-old and I arrived at Children's Medical Center fifteen minutes early.

It was a day I'll never forget.

The TV in the waiting room, perched high and out of reach, was tuned in to the news. There were no toys, no books, and no snack machines.

We were told to wait. So we waited. And waited. For an hour we waited. About the time I started to feel sorry for my insurance carrier, the receptionist sent us back to a small, sterile exam room. There we waited and waited and waited. After another hour, the doctor appeared.

Within ten minutes of interacting with Jonathan, the doctor turned to me and announced, "He sure is a smart, little guy. He's different, too. Yep, he'll probably always be different."

"But, but, but," I stammered, openmouthed, "aren't there tests? Can't you hook his brain up to something and take a picture?"

"I *could* do tests," the doctor said, already moving toward the door, "but it would tell me what I just told you, that parts of his brain are different."

Well, duh! I thought, eyes wide with disbelief, I'd been saying my son was different for two years. It was the only sure thing I knew.

"What do I do now?" I asked, still hopeful for an answer.

"Call me if you ever need to consider drugs."

Then I said, feeling oh so foolish, "Okay. Thanks a lot. See ya later."

P.S. Please don't use my experience with a pediatric neurologist as an excuse not to see one. Your child's issues are unique. In most cases, it is essential for insight. Also, your insurance company might need their input to justify other tests or treatments.

TAKE-WITH

Looking back on that appointment, I can only shake my head. *Wanting* answers wasn't the problem. It's the *getting them* that proved to be so difficult. I also wasn't prepared for any part of that day, the wait, the exam or the results.

Here's what I did learn.

I learned to take snacks and toys to all appointments. I learned to promise a reward for good behavior. I learned that I'm not always going to get a *take-with*, my word for any helpful piece of information that can push me along in the fight for my child's best. I learned it wasn't going to be easy.

And now, looking back, I learned that doctors don't have all the answers. It was up to me to work harder to find them.

WHERE DO YOU GO FOR ANSWERS?

An April, 2001, article in a national parenting magazine said this to parents of *different* children. "Your pediatrician is your first line of defense." It went on to say something to the effect that parents could count on their child's doctor to provide a diagnosis, then lead them to a cure.

In the safety of my room, I polished off a scathing letter to the editor, which I never sent of course, crying, "No!"

Jonathan's first pediatrician gave me only two pieces of advice on the subject of my son's differences:

"Well, at least he's not worse," and, when I suggested nutritional testing to look for answers, he said, "you know I don't believe in that stuff."

If my own child's doctor and a fancy brain doctor couldn't tell me what to do, who could? Thank goodness we found our way to a supportive pediatrician who was just as eager as I to find the answers.

TIME TO GO TO WORK

You are here because something's not quite right. You've chosen to find answers, even if they mean change and the unknown, because it means your child's future will be brighter.

It's time to say good-bye to your comfort zone and go to work. First, research your professional resources. There are many wonderful physicians who specialize in *different*. Find one. At the same time, begin testing your child, which you can do on your own, to find out what common sense things can help right now.

Again, our goal right now isn't so much to find a label, but to find out what's wrong, then see what we can do to help.

FIND A DOCTOR

The Pediatrician

Most of us already have a pediatrician. But is it the *right* pediatrician? Perhaps your pediatrician has taken care of your family for generations, or they're a close friend. Maybe they came highly recommended by *Good Housekeeping* or by mothers on your block.

But your child is *different*. It's especially important, in your case, to have a pediatrician who will encourage your curiosity and persistence, your willingness to learn more about your child. You should feel comfortable talking honestly about what's going on at home. It should be someone who treats you credibly as you tell them what you're learning (much of which will be new to them because they didn't take a class in NOT NORMAL at med school). Finally, you need a doctor who can freely admit they don't have all the answers and does not feel threatened every time you ask for an unfamiliar test.

This is a partnership. You are both learning. You need their advice and they need to learn from you. The old school thought of, "I'm the doctor and I don't like to be questioned," is not for you and your different child.

Don't be hurt or surprised at resistance. When asking for referrals and tests, remind yourself you're an intelligent, practical person taking proactive steps toward helping your child. You're brilliant, not silly. If the doctor says, "No, I don't believe in that kind of stuff," find a pediatrician who will support you in your quest to help your child.

Here's a heads-up: For this journey, it is possible to know more than your pediatrician about the latest discoveries regarding your child's differences. It's even possible to disagree with your pediatrician. **Begin with your pediatrician, but do not wait on your pediatrician.**

Visit a Developmental Pediatrician

If your child is pre-school or younger, it's important to see a developmental pediatrician, specially trained to understand your child's development, i.e., the skills they should have at their specific age. An assessment by a developmental pediatrician is like getting a baseline in behavior. It might answer some of your questions or even add a few to your list.

At another mother's recommendation, I made an appointment with Dr. Wonderful (my name for her), the resident developmental pediatrician for Easter Seals. She observed the same weaknesses I'd seen, but also pointed out several wonderful things about my son. She gave me a name to describe Jonathan's differences, one I'd never heard, some reading material and best of all, a written plan of action.

Dr. Wonderful was very gentle and careful with her words, a lesson I learned to apply to my own dealings when another mom came calling.

"Now, it's not *this*," I remember her saying, "and it could be *this*, but I can tell that Jonathan is very smart, and he's still very young. So here's what you can do to help him along."

"First," she said, "it's very important to get him into a structured program."

"Second, continue speech therapy and find some kind of fine-motor therapy." Finally, she said, "It's going to be okay."

Finding a Special Doctor

If you have the good fortune of spotting a child similar to yours, ask the parent if they see a certain doctor. Other mothers love sharing joyful information such as a great doctor.

Many of the books in the Resources section include web sites or actual doctors in this field who can then refer you to a doctor in your area. It is not unusual to have to travel. Many families travel across country for that first consultation, and then communicate by phone. Think out of the box.

Testing can be done on your own, but if you can find a doctor who has made it his calling to handle patients like your child, grab hold of them. You might save some money, time and effort.

With or without a doctor, I can't emphasize enough the importance of moving ahead. The younger your child, the better chance of repairing the things that aren't working right.

There's lots to be done, so with questions in hand, with or without a doctor holding your hand, start with the obvious.

TESTING

This is a broad overview of testing for your child's differences. It's intentionally simple because I think having the big picture helps you see the end, and that's motivating!

> Please remember, I am neither a doctor nor a therapist. This is my own logical, oversimplified way of discussing steps to take toward understanding the differences in your child. Neither is this an exhaustive list of tests.

PART I, THE PHYSICAL

Hearing and Vision

Your child's hearing and vision are easily checked, so you might be surprised to find out that Clarence or Zoe has a simple problem, easily fixed. Your public school should have a system in place for testing preschool age children and your pediatrician will be able to refer you to resources. Test until you're satisfied you've done everything you can to understand your child's "hardware".

Consider This

Some children (and adults) have perfect vision, yet light (certain colors, florescent, stronger degrees) bothers them. In 1983, a man named Irlen discovered that tinted lenses helped certain problems, particularly coordination, balance, mood, etc. He saw the greatest improvement in children with dyslexia. These glasses are called *Irlen lenses* and are prescribed by specialists.

Speech, Occupational and Physical Therapy

If physical problems such as balance, fine-motor skills, and/or language problems exist, more testing is needed. Again, the school, doctor's office and other mothers are great resources for finding help in this area. The sooner, the better.

Sometimes, the issues are intertwined. Lack of speech can be the result of a hearing problem. Or, the child may have poor muscle tone or sensory issues. No matter the magnitude of issues, the obvious ones are a great way to begin.

NOTE: Just like facing doubts and fears about your child's normalcy is huge, admitting you need a *therapist* can be just as hard. Please, don't let pride slow you down from seeking help. *Run, don't walk*, to your nearest therapist. I've never met a family that regretted seeking help. What I *have* seen is the relief in a parent's eyes as they watch their child receive the help they need.

Sensory Integration Therapy

A majority of different children have some type of sensory dysfunction. For example: A child hates the feel of clothes, screams when you brush their hair, slouches in their chair or seems tired all the time, they run from loud noises or need to constantly chew or move, just to stay focused. They either need revving up or calming down.

While not new, sensory integration therapy is still relatively unknown among the mainstream medical community. Why, I don't know. It is one of the handful of things we did that helped our child the most, resulting not only in physical improvement (improved fine motor and muscle tone), but also behavioral improvement. Jonathan went from spending a rather short amount of time in the classroom because of discipline problems, to all day without any major interruptions.

In a nutshell, Sensory Integration stimulates the brain through physical movement. It helps the brain become more organized and calmer. It is not coordination- or play-therapy and the apparatus used is quite different from traditional physical and occupational therapy.

I know children formally labeled bad, bored, and disruptive, who are now happy, challenged and cooperative. I highly recommend looking into it, and yes, a child can be evaluated up front to see if this type of therapy would benefit them.

PART II, BEHAVIORAL

Driving Blind

As a *mature* single, I finally realized my honeymoon in New England might never happen. So, in 1984, I took matters into my own hands and moved! I packed my car, said good-bye to life in Texas and drove twelve hundred miles to a city I'd never been to: Boston, Massachusetts.

Did you know Boston is on the water? I didn't.

Every day was an adventure, and somehow I managed to survive. After two interesting years, I fit all of what was left of my possessions into two suitcases, flew home and started over.

I admit I'm unlike most people. I appreciate the adage that *ignorance is bliss*. I also live by *when in doubt, make a decision*. Many would disagree and thank goodness for that. But don't you think there are times in life when we have no other choice but to drive blindly, for the simple reason it's better than doing nothing?

This next section will feel like you're driving blind because the answers lie at the end of the process. In other words, you make the appointment, pay for the testing, follow through on the therapy, and then find out if any of it works.

Sometimes you see results within days or sometimes within a month. Sometimes it just wasn't what your child needed.

The best advice I can give you when trying to decide about a mode of treatment, is to trust your instincts, do your homework, talk to people with firsthand experience, and get your most reliable information from watching your child. (They're your best laboratory.)

NOW, WHY AM I THE POINT MAN?

Didn't I mention this at the beginning? Most differences are helped by YOU doing the work. It just doesn't happen unless you get out there, learn the game, call the plays, and run the bases.

Translation? You do the research, networking, order the tests, and follow through on treatment.

Again, why? Because things will get better for your child if you are helping them. So get back out there!

The Body/Brain Connection

Why do doctors tell pregnant mothers to eat with their baby in mind? Broccoli, flax, vitamins, etc., but once that baby is born, they say nutrition (or the condition of any of the bodies' systems) has little to do with brain function?

I wondered, too. Following the example of many others, I started helping Jonathan's body. I now have proof the health of the body (and its different systems) impacts the brain's ability to function.

The immune system, the digestive system, and the nervous system play a critical role in helping the brain know what to do. If any part of this concert of instruments is out of tune, the results can be disastrous. Here's where we need science (testing) to help us get inside the body to understand what might possibly need help.

Immune system

"I can't emphasize enough that the brain does not function in isolation. It is a team player; it needs vital nutrients as well as

informational input. To fill these needs the brain depends heavily on complex interactions between the immune, endocrine, and gastrointestinal systems." *Children With Starving Brains*, page 38, by Jacqueline McCandless, MD.

The immune system does so much more than ward off colds or help the body recover from a tonsillectomy. It is constantly at work, responding to outside poisons in the air, our food and even poisons our own body produces. When not working well, all kinds of physical problems can occur, often resulting in behavioral problems.

If a child exhibits immune system problems, consider an immunological work-up, through an independent lab or your doctor. It's expensive, and you will need a doctor's help to read the test; however, it's full of information and answers about your child's immune system.

Assess your own child's immune system. Do they get sick easily? Have they been on antibiotics regularly? Do they have skin rashes, severe allergies or asthma? With or without formal testing, it's a good sign you need to bolster their immune system.

For almost two years, Jonathan had ear infections, one after the other. There was always a bottle of the *pink stuff* in our refrigerator before graduating to the more powerful *white stuff*. Without knowing it, we were weakening his immune system with every teaspoonful.

I also assumed, wrongly so, that when the infection was gone, it meant my son was healthy. Instead, the continuous antibiotics, along with an already poor diet, damaged his immune system.

For us, taking probiotics to bolster the good bacteria (available at most health food stores) eliminated a chronic yeast infection (and he was *suddenly* potty-trained), and Jonathan no longer came down with seasonal chest infections. His allergies also improved.

NOTE: There are different grades of probiotics. The best ones have the most live viruses and are refrigerated. See Resources section.

Another pleasant result of adding the probiotics was a happier child. It makes sense that if you don't feel well, you don't behave well. Only after helping Jonathan's immune system did we realize how poor he must have been feeling.

Digestive System

"Research has shown that 60-70% of the immune system in humans is located within the intestinal tract and its digestive organs, easily making the gut the largest immune system organ in the body." *Children With Starving Brains*, page 89.

As Jonathan's behaviors worsened, I remembered hearing about food sensitivities, but the thought of a list of *Don'ts* in the kitchen kept me from asking any more questions. Then I learned that "food sensitivity" didn't just mean an allergic reaction. It referred to foods that affect behavior, language development, auditory processing, etc. I had to look further.

Testing through an independent lab (a simple urine sample) revealed that Jonathan was not digesting gluten and casein (grains and dairy). Instead, they acted like a drug, keeping his brain from functioning as it should. Removing those foods was the first thing that put Jonathan on the road back to Normal. Changing our kitchen around was a small lifestyle change compared to the dramatic improvement it made in our lives.

(Adding Enzymes and L-Glutamin, a gut-healer, helped Jonathan's digestion even more.)

Testing the urine can also reveal serious fungal, bacterial and viral problems in the digestive system. Gut bugs like clostridia and candida can cause diarrhea, (painful) constipation and bad behavior. These can often be cleaned up with probiotics (good bacteria).

The beauty of a digestive problem is that simple testing can often reveal the problems and then, under a doctor's care or on your own, you can start helping your child feel better, possibly for the first time in their lives. **If the digestive system isn't working right, don't expect behaviors to be normal.**

Nervous System

If you think I've oversimplified things up until now, listen to this. I picture the nervous system as a set of complex telephone lines to the brain. If a line isn't healthy, the signals will be faulty. Here's what you can do to help.

1. Ensure a good night's sleep. The body repairs itself at night, repairing the nervous system last. Only a few hours of deep sleep means the nervous system goes un-repaired.

2. Sixty percent of the brain needs essential fatty acids (DHA). Infants especially need the right fats to develop normally. Don't ignore the bad fats (white bread, chips, fries, etc.) anymore in your child's diet! The brain will pull from these faulty fats if the good fats aren't available, creating lousy connections in the brain. The brain cannot function normally without the right fats.

3. Consider a virus. Viruses live in the nervous system. When you come under stress, your nerves weaken and the virus rears its ugly head, for example, as a cold sore or imbalance. That's because the virus, living in the nerves, is able to attack. Under a doctor's care, you may treat the virus with antivirals.

   (This mode of treatment for differences is still new to me and I have not personally experienced using antivirals to treat developmental differences. But it does sound logical, it's noninvasive and I personally know people helped by this treatment.)

Test the Nutritional Status of the Body.

What does your child's physical body need? Perhaps their thyroid is out of whack. Or, during tests for digestive problems you found other missing elements. Deficiencies (especially in the brain) in any one of several areas can mean the difference in a child being able to tie their shoes or read a book.

Following the advice found in several of the books in the Resources section, I gave my son a multi-vitamin (from Kirkman Labs), extra B6, zinc, calcium, magnesium and essential fatty acids, to name just a few. Jonathan made incredible leaps in speech, logic, reasoning, and comprehension. I know it sounds too easy, too simple. Take it from hundreds of parents like myself; it's the basics that count. Read the material. Look at the studies.

If you give your child's body (brain) what it needs, they will probably get better. Learn about this as fast as you can because it is the easiest, most productive method of treatment, if it's what your child needs. It's logical, noninvasive and there are hundreds of parents to vouch for the positive effects. Those three reasons should hurl you on to the biological bandwagon.

MORE BAND-AIDS

Now that you're on the war path, determined to find answers, you'll no doubt be charging blindly into your own world of adventure, and so I present the following cheat sheet for the inevitable frustration.

CHARGE!

You will feel overwhelmed, I guarantee it. It takes a long time to process all this new information, but you will eventually absorb and understand it.

Expect extra phone calls and paperwork and "our next opening is in two months" because it's the system we live in. Expect "*you're* responsible for the referral from your doctor," and "now, why exactly are you here?" Expect an occasional "there's nothing I can do for you.*" Remember, some still haven't heard.

Try to save phone calls to your insurance company and doctor's office for later in the week. You'll avoid the longer holds. Always get a name. Make a record of phone calls. Try to develop a relationship with someone in the claims department.

Keep your insurance card, along with social security numbers, with you at all times.

Be prepared for long waits. The waiting room becomes a jail sentence when trapped with a child who can't sit still. Pack a bag with activities to occupy your child for at least two hours. Always take a snack. Think about offering a reward for good behavior.

At almost every initial visit, I was asked to fill out a questionnaire with lots of "when did he," questions. I wish I'd had a cheat sheet with all those firsts written down: first crawl, first walk, first words, how *many* words, first problems, etc.

Take your written list of questions to each appointment.

Start a notebook. Take notes. At some point, you'll begin losing test results, progress reports, etc. It's wonderful looking back to see how far you've come. Look forward to the opportunity to show a few early doomsayers how wrong they turned out to be.

Keep a copy of everything.

Adapt to waiting room etiquette. If TV helps, use it. If it's blaring the Weather Channel, explain your situation to others watching, and change the channel! You **can** take walks in the hall. Ask for the first appointment of the day, or first opening after lunch. Waits are less likely. Try your best to leave other children at home.

Be bold with the doctor. Well-meaning physicians don't always have the answers, but don't be afraid to ask.

Be prepared for accidents. Keep an extra set of clothes with you.

Expect to have to listen. You might have seen only the tiniest of symptoms. While someone is telling you how to treat a manic depressive, you are heading for the nearest exit. **Stop: Listen to the seeds of what they're saying.** What are they doing that's good for their kid? You might have the advantage of a lesser evil now, but something they say might be helpful in the future.

As the days turn into months and the months turn into years, remind yourself that you are doing **all you know to do** at this stage, at your level of understanding. Don't wait too long to begin the process of testing your child, even though it feels like you're driving blind. You are doing what you should be doing—something.

READY OR NOT

The next chapter is a landscape of labels, painted with a very broad brush.

To Skip or Not to Skip

Many of you want to know what *It* is, but <u>without</u> the label. You want someone to explain your child, who, by the way, has more layers than a sweet vidalia onion. Just, please, nobody call it an onion. If that's you, skip the next chapter.

Others, however, want to know what to call *It*. You're looking for a handle to hold on to. You're ready for a label.

Like a Monet, this next chapter paints an impression of what several labels look like. I ask that you forgive me, again, for the oversimplification. But so much of attaching labels is generalization and variation. It's common sense and observation, not an exact science. It's also what women are really good at—discernment, perception and intuition. Or, simply put, what we see, feel and know.

CHAPTER FIVE

Labels
You Gotta Love 'Em

LABELS MAKE GOOD HANDLES

I felt the first icy chill of a label when Jonathan's grandmother innocently suggested Jonathan might have autism. I reared up, claws extended, pushed my baby behind me, and bared my teeth.

Do I understand what it is to be afraid of a label? Yes.

In my defense, I had a good excuse for hating that label. In 1996, there were many societal signs that a child with ADD or ADHD was acceptable. But words like Asperger's syndrome and autism? Not one bit. It was as good as a death sentence. Few people, and even fewer doctors, knew that both were treatable. No wonder I was afraid.

WHY LABELS?

Whether we like them or not, labels are tools. They often spark the birth of something wonderful, and then guide us through the maze of discovery and treatment. They are the beginning, never the ending. In this chapter, I hope to give you enough reason to investigate the possibility that your child might have a label. (I only cover four, so please look beyond this narrow scope if necessary.)

Labels make good handles to mentally hang those emotions on. They can bring peace. In my own experience, having a word for my son's behaviors was a great relief. Maybe because I'd struggled to avoid any label for so long. Or maybe because I didn't fully understand what the label meant (the 'ignorance is bliss' position). Either way, we all breathed a sigh of relief with those first words for the unknown.

A label helps to focus your energies. Like any good researcher, you must start with an assumption. The wrong label will rule itself out in time.

A label will help pinpoint information and resources for treatment, as well as support from other families just like yours.

LABELS ARE FOR OTHERS, AS WELL

It never fails. At the beginning of summer camp and the school year alike, there comes a cry from the head office: "Please label your children's things!"

I try, but by the end of the year, I'm the mom buried under gummy lunchboxes and stinky socks in the lost and found closet. All because I hate to label!

I still bristle with the memory of notes sent home from my infant daughter's babysitter. *Please label*!, written in red, would be taped to the top of her sippee cup, or filter down from the folds of her diaper bag. I understood the purpose but hated the exercise.

With our different children, it's the same thing. Not only do labels help us, they help others as well.

Explaining *different* to friends, family and teachers is frustrating, at best. It reminds me of a friend's prediction concerning swimming pool maintenance. He said, "For the first six months, you'll struggle with the brushes and chemicals, then you'll hire a pool service like everybody else." The same is true with a label. After spending a few years trying to explain *different*, you'll probably come to the same conclusion I did. A label saves time and confusion.

For any kind of outside help, the label often determines services. You want your child's needs and the services he receives to match.

BECAUSE IT JUST IS

Having said all that, I understand the conflict of explaining your child with one word. Labeling boils down to a necessary evil: imperfect and incomplete, filled with nuances and certain shadowy signs but having a purpose all its own.

WHAT LABELS ARE NOT

One Thing

In the movie *City Slickers*, Billy Crystal plays a dissatisfied, aging, tired-of-Corporate-America kind of guy. He and two similarly dissatisfied friends escape to the Wild Wild West to herd cattle; in essence, to find themselves.

Jack Palance is the consummate don't-mess-with-me-or-you're-dead trail boss. In a heart-to-heart talk, Palance tells Crystal that finding happiness is all about *one thing*.

"What one thing?" asks Crystal.

Palance holds up his index finger and repeats the answer, "one thing".

"What's the one thing?" begs Crystal, looking at his own finger.

"That's what you've got to figure out," answers Palance. Billy Crystal spends the rest of the movie trying to do just that.

Okay, maybe that's true for men avoiding a mid-life crisis, but it is certainly not true for different children. If there's one thing I've learned while watching different children over the last ten years, it's that often there is no single diagnosis and certainly, no single fix.

Being different is not about one thing. It's not just a speech delay, or one little obsessive behavior. I wish we could just agree to label our problems *Processing Disorders*, as coined by one doctor. (We'd all fit under that umbrella!)

But that's in the future. Today, we have cubbyhole names for our *different* differences. It's called a diagnosis.

Set in Stone

You've started with the obvious and already moved on to investigating the possibilities. So, you say, you've tried changing the diet. Suddenly, behaviors change! Then, you discover, the brain needs some nutrients so you add a few supplements. All of a sudden, reading and speech improve. But still, there are more issues.

So, you go back and do a little tweaking with cranial sacral therapy or neurofeedback or homeopathy. Or maybe you take time off from any therapy when, Oh my heavens, suddenly they hit puberty and what was that? Strange behaviors are popping out all over. So now you decide a little social training will help. Perhaps a drug works best.

Your child is certainly not the same child today that they were when you started. The diagnosis may become narrower, or it may broaden as you learn more.

Not As Bad As You Think

As a child, I specifically remember what it was like to drive to my grandmother's house. In my little mind, it was at least two towns away. In fact, I would lie down in the back of the car to take a nap, because it took so long and was so far away.

A few years later, I discovered something. My grandmother lived less than ten miles away and we went through two shopping centers (the two towns) to get there. It took about fifteen minutes.

My perspective of the problem changed as my understanding matured.

As you learn more about your child's differences, your perspective will change. The problems will change, what you perceive as good and bad will change, and what you think is important will change. Yes, they will.

IN MY OPINION

The dialogue that best describes the *different* child is Autism Spectrum Disorder, with a strong emphasis on Spectrum.

Picture a long two-by-four of chicken-scratch with little marks up and down the board, from beginning to end. Your child is one of those marks. Mine's on there. My husband is on there. Happy people with families and businesses are on there.

Each mark is a place of neurological precision or lack thereof. At the far end are the Rain Men of this world, the savants, the nonverbal. Following down the board, in no specific order, are the cases of mild autism and pervasive developmental disorders, ADD and ADHD, (Attention Deficit [Hyperactive] Disorder), and Asperger's syndrome. At the bottom of our board are speech, coordination and reading problems.

This is the Autism Spectrum, a rainbow of colorful differences that many, many people reside along. Sometimes it's a clear label, often a combination of several. But they all involve the brain. They all involve some quirk in the way the brain *processes* information.

GOOD COMPANY

People with Autism Spectrum Disorder are in good company. I know of several successful computer magnates who fit nicely on this scale. Many adults have lived their entire lives without realizing they even have the disorder, though they are familiar with the struggle it takes to compensate for their differences. A certain relief comes when they realize, perhaps for the first time, there was a reason for their struggles to get through high school and college, or to fit into adult society.

> *I understand that many will disagree with my inclusion of ADD and ADHD as an Autism Spectrum Disorder. We'll just have to agree to disagree. Again, I wish we simply used the label Processing Disorder; but that is not yet the case.*

AUTISM? ASPERGERS? ADHD? ADD?

☒ Show me a normal kid and I'll show you Aspergers with the right medication.

☒ Show me a nice quiet kid and I'll show you high-functioning autism.

☒ Show me a rail-thin teenager taking medication for ADD and I'll show you Asperger's syndrome on the wrong medication.

☒ A quick-witted chatterbox who can't live with dead air? ADD/ADHD or maybe just a very verbal child.

I know all these children. I knew them before they had a label and after they had labels. I knew them when their labels changed. For some, their labels are still changing.

My point is that labels are the thin layer of ice covering an ocean of differences. Even as you search for information that will most surely tell you *what* your child is, remember, it's more important to understand *who* your child is.

Following are a layman's list of common behaviors for children with autism spectrum disorder, and more specifically, ADD, ADHD, Asperger's syndrome and autism.

Attention Deficit Disorder - "Hello!"

Looks like this: Has trouble focusing, a poor self-starter, easily distracted, rarely completes more than one task without needing a prompt, forgetful. Can't see what's right in front of them, often has a noticeable tick—this can be a rapid, repetitive movement, often done while trying to concentrate; rarely finishes a task (homework) because they can't see they're not finished, the meaning 'done' is unclear, slow reader, poor handwriting, revved up - impacts handwriting and reading (seems like they have a learning disability but disappears or greatly improves with medication).

Attention Deficit Hyperactive Disorder - "Does that kid ever sit still?" (A disorder of extremes)

Looks like this: ADD with a twist. Trouble sitting still, short attention span or hyperfocused - obsessive, easily distracted, demanding, excitable, cries easily, gets wound up easily, then crashes, has trouble keeping his hands to himself, plays too rough, breaks things a lot. Visual and auditory problems, motor coordination, attention/memory problems, sensory integration dysfunction. When physically tired becomes even more revved up.

Asperger's Syndrome - "He's very intelligent but in a quirky sort of way."

Looks like this: Normal to above average I.Q. Early reader. Enjoys sharing his knowledge with others, often at the expense of normal conversation. Doesn't naturally understand the flow of conversation. Will interrupt, blurt out odd statements, talk about themselves. Very literal, difficulty with intuition, reading between the lines. Depression, mood swings (often caused by a nutritional imbalance). Digestive issues. Stresses out easily. Poor social skills, but can learn. Peer relationships poor. Very comfortable with computers. Avoids eye contact. No significant delay in language or age-appropriate self-help skills. Loves rules, structure, but hates too long of a to-do list. Can complete tasks.

Autism - "Happy to be Alone"

Some skills (motor) develop normally while others (language) are impaired. Can be brilliant, absent-minded, a little awkward physically, poor fine-motor or muscle tone (muscle dyspraxia), early reader but has a different way of using language. Poor understanding of pragmatics (joking, kidding, in jest). Awkward eye contact, sensory integration dysfunction (noise, light, textures). Poor peer relationships. Needs help in re-directing when unhappy. Enjoys structure, will complete tasks, enjoys appropriate responsibilities, poor social skills, loves routine, hates change, possible auditory processing problems, cognitive problems (abstract concepts).

This may be the closest you've come to deciding on a label. Just remember, that's not the important part of your job. That would be helping a child reach their greatest potential. Whether it's a touch of ADD or slam-dunk autism, differences respond to treatment, and it's never too late to begin.

CHAPTER SIX

To School or Not to School

All of thy children shall be taught of the Lord; and great shall be the peace of thy children. Isaiah 54:13.

SCHOOLS

I can still feel the burst of peace that flooded over me when that developmental pediatrician pulled out pen and paper and wrote:

#1) Continue speech therapy, and

#2) find a structured program as soon as possible.

Even at three, she said, *Jonathan will benefit from several hours of structure* versus the few truly structured minutes I provided at home.

Now it's your turn to do the same. (Yes, even if they're only three.) You've already made a mental leap from normal to different, with giant leaps from different to testing to therapy.

Now it's time to make another courageous jump. From private testing and therapy, to programs that aren't just thirty minutes long, and a place where you're not in charge. Your child is ready for a more structured setting—school.

CITY RESOURCES

Thankfully, the school system agrees it's a big leap for our different kids to join the educational system. To help, many cities provide a program to help prepare children for kindergarten. A diagnosis is not required. The school system does its own readiness testing. In our case, Jonathan qualified for in-home services. (Look at it like a personal trainer for free!) We received general play therapy to stimulate speech and interaction skills.

If this is an option for you, ask that your child receive the maximum amount of help offered. Twice a week? Take it. Three times a week? Even better. This isn't the time to be shy. Ask yourself this question: Can a child improve too fast? I don't think so.

THE SCHOOL SYSTEM

At age four, our school system stepped in to help. Their purpose is to help ready the child for kindergarten. It is not therapy, but can include speech and OT. This program is generally referred to as an early childhood program. It provides the welcome structure for a different child using materials and resources you will appreciate as well as a much-needed break for you. There is also valuable social interaction and stimulation.

GUILT ATTACK!

What? Put my child into someone else's care? They don't know him! They don't understand him! They don't *luuuv* him!

I felt every one of those things, so here are the facts about what's really going on.

GUILT-FREE FACTS

If Clarence or Zoe need help, you need help.

Give the school system credit for wanting to help enhance your child's readiness to learn. They have years of experience along with feedback from mothers just like you. Every year they work with kids like Clarence. They know a lot of good things that you don't know. Trust me, nothing will surprise them.

A structured program will challenge, direct and facilitate your child's learning in ways you can't.

I'm sorry, but your child needs others to be involved in their lives. *Especially* if that child is different.

We've already agreed you don't have all the answers. Start learning what the professionals know.

It's not guilt, it's fear. Don't be afraid to put Zoe into someone else's care for a few hours a day. One day at a time.

*Give your child the chance to be challenged. They will **always** surprise you.*

I dreaded Jonathan's first day of an early childhood program. So how was it? He loved it! He couldn't wait to go back. He was so happy with all the materials they had for him to play with. They had a predictable schedule with music, art, reading, play, etc. Suddenly I felt guilty for not sending him sooner.

The school also offered bus service. "Forget it," I said. "Put my baby on a bus?"

Again, I was wrong. When he saw everyone else get off the bus at school, it was very clear to me that he would be riding the bus from then on.

PUBLIC OR PRIVATE?

The real issue isn't public or private. It's finding a place where you and the teacher work *together*. Unlike 'normal' kids, where school is school and home is home, our different kids need structure and consistency all day long. Maybe they just need extra help to 'keep up'. It's essential that you and your school consistently talk about what the other is doing, that you are in agreement and are committed to supporting one another.

If, at home, you are working on helping your child speak clearly, they should be doing the same at school. You should use the same words when disciplining ("hitting hurts") and goals agreed upon. This applies to any school situation.

The Public System

You will soon learn that the public system is bound by very strict guidelines. You'll become familiar with the ARD (Admission, Review, Dismissal) and IEP (Individualized Education Plan). You might hire an advocate to help support you when certain expectations are not being met.

It's hard to know what is best for your child and therefore hard to know what to fight for. Looking back, I highly recommend joining any kind of support group with mothers ahead of you in the system. Keep your expectations high. Work hard to stay in touch with your child's teacher and visit often.

There are talented and dedicated teachers in the public school system. You can make it work. You may not have a choice, though I've heard of many families that hear of a good program in another district and actually move, lock, stock and barrel.

Once the decision is made, public or private, get ready for an incredible moment.

As on Jonathan's first day of the early childhood program, I dreaded his official first day of kindergarten at the new school. I knew it would take only one enormous scream or kick to the shin for me to get the phone call, "Come get this kid!"

I watched Jonathan go inside. Suddenly, I rushed in after him. "Listen, Mr. Teacher," I said, "did I tell you that sometimes Jonathan can scream really loud? Oh, and one more thing, did I tell you he might hit you, too?"

"No problem," the teacher smiled. "Have a nice day."

As I floated back to my car, I had this amazing feeling. I was free for a few hours because someone else was prepared to understand my child and to work with him. Not only would Jonathan be safe, understood and loved, they were going to help *me*. That's what a school is for and I believe there is a place like that for you.

GET READY

The next two chapters concern the physically violent child. This does not apply to everyone, but because it was so much a part of my life for several years, I must present something to those who might need to know there is help and hope along this difficult road.

CHAPTER SEVEN

Let's Get Physical: Defense

PART I

Dedication: All I have are words, but to those who have a story, I honor you. You are nothing less than heroic. And you are survivors. These next two chapters are for you.

Note: No matter what you think is different about your child, if they are unusually violent, I hope you'll search tirelessly for the cause. The gluten-free/casein-free diet immediately ended almost all of Jonathan's severe tantrums. The solution may be different for you, but I believe there is something to provide relief for all.

At the central core of my being is an unshakable belief in the love between mother and child. The kind of love that nothing can change, no matter how far one might drift from "like" or how wildly the oats are sown, it's still there. It's fact. It will always be.

But one day, maybe like you, I found myself in possession of a child I was completely unprepared for. One day I realized my child didn't look deeply into my eyes; he had no words to draw us together or say *I'm glad you're here* by some touch or glance. I felt separated from him. *He needs me for so little*, I often thought.

Still, I needed to believe he loved me and, without question, I loved him.

Life grew harder as Jonathan went from age four to five to six. As though the sadness of having a child who's different, (one who confounds you every day with their quirky habits and demands), weren't enough, Jonathan was physically violent. I tried so hard to understand.

First, I pretended we were just a different version of normal; but, as Jonathan grew, so did the violence and I remember those early years by their anger and sadness. One day, though, I saw something new, and it changed everything.

When Jonathan was about four or five, a violent episode began, as it often did. I said "No," he threw something, and the hitting began.

Clumsily, I tried to stop him. Like a caged animal trying to escape, the blows kept coming. I shouted at Jonathan to stop. I'm not sure if I was angrier at the pain or the fact that he had *the nerve*.

In the next instant, I caught his eye, and for the first time I *saw* what he was thinking. It was a blow, straight to my heart.

"He's fighting for his life," I sobbed that night to my husband, Bill, "and I'm the enemy! He doesn't even act like I'm his mother or that I love him."

My own words helped me realize something. **Jonathan was reacting to my anger, not ME**. I turned the corner from feeling sorry for myself, that this was all about ME, to having a new compassion for Jonathan. Every scream was a cry for help and as his mother, I heard it like a shrill call to arms—to do everything in my power to help him.

For me, it began with looking for help. Life had become miserable, and the future? We tried not to think about it. Suddenly, I was hungry for information. No treatment, no diagnosis, no avenue of therapy, could be any worse than what I was living with every day. It was time to quit being an amateur and tackle the world of developmental differences.

What about all those years in the trenches? I spent them without a plan. I didn't know how to defend myself or how to help Jonathan through the worst parts. I needed someone to show me how to handle a violent child.

TIME OUT

If this scenario fits your family, I know it's hard to talk about. If I were to ask for a show of hands, would I get even one? I doubt it. But between these pages, there is secrecy. No one is reading your mind.

Just in case you are feeling like you should be excused from the room, I've got that covered, too. Here are a few of the excuses I used during those difficult years.

"Not My Child!"

I preferred the "wait and see" approach to this whole mess of having a different child. A lot of my friends liked it, too. But not my brilliant husband. *He* had to bring home reams of dialogue off a web site. He had to buy books that talked about extremely scary stuff.

Talk to the hand, I'd say. So what if Jonathan doesn't talk as well as he should? *So what if he has a few other delays?* "This isn't Jonathan," I'd insist, as his helpful information landed in the trash.

That was a dreadful mistake. When life shifted into crisis mode, I had no clue where to begin. By the time I was desperate for help, so much damage had been done; to our hearts, our home, and our other kids.

Navigating back to Normal took a lot longer than it could have, and the rough years in between broke about every pretty thing I had.

"I've Already Talked to my Pediatrician"

The day Jonathan saw me as the enemy, I realized I didn't know my son.

Was he afraid? Hurting? How could I help him understand that he wasn't trapped or caged? What was going on in his brain that made him want to hurt me? What could I do? I went to the only person I knew to ask.

"There's nothing you can do," the doctor said. "Just be glad he isn't worse." Talk about a feeling of failure!

So we continued to 'handle' things on our own. It was much later that I learned there were answers even my pediatrician didn't know about.

"I Don't Want to Talk About It!"

The movie *Cold Comfort Farm* is a dark comedy with all sorts of strange characters. Seven adults (including four grown children) are doomed to live on the family farm, simply because the old and decrepit grandmother of the family shouts "No one ever leaves Cold Comfort Farm!" every time someone walks by her bedroom door.

And then one day, a sophisticated niece from London arrives, determined to improve their lot. Eventually, she confronts the old matriarch.

"Why," she calls through the barred door, "can't anyone leave the farm?"

The voice we hear is raspy and cruel. "Because I saw something *naaahhhsty* in the woodshed."

The family members nod knowingly, having heard this all their lives.

To everyone's surprise, the niece asks again. "Well, what did you see? What was so nasty in the woodshed?"

The rest of the family, eyes wide with terror, lean in close to hear the answer.

The heavy oak door is silent until Grandmother's voice, like gravel shouts, "I said I saw something *naaahhhsty* in the woodshed!"

"But what was it?" her niece asks again.

We are all holding our breath until *finally* Grandmother answers some-what meekly, "I don't remember, but whatever it was, it was nasty."

It's a turning point in the movie. What has hung over the family like a shroud of death for three generations is lifted. Sunlight, for the first time, shines on the scene, people smile, they start taking baths, the cows give milk, etc.

Handling a difficult child is something you do want to talk about. You want to talk to other mothers that understand what you're saying. You have to trust that I understand what it's like to hide behind the door, as well as all the effort it takes to keep others out because it is so terribly nasty. I hope this chapter allows glorious sunlight to break through.

"It's None of My Business"

Over coffee, a friend was telling me about her encounter with an acquaintance, whom, she observed, must be a new mother because of the tiny baby in her arms. A mother of two young boys herself, my friend guessed the child to be about two months old. She went on to tell me how surprised she was to find that the baby was, in fact, over nine months old. The baby's mother tearfully shared how they had just learned the infant had a rare disorder.

As we talked, my friend relayed how, at the time, she immediately thought of another family facing the same dilemma. Fortunately, this other family had received the diagnosis shortly after birth, sought treatment and seen some wonderful results.

In the shadow of a Starbuck's awning, my friend debated over whether or not she should pass along phone numbers. *Wouldn't she be stepping on someone's privacy,* she wondered out loud? Mightn't it make someone feel uncomfortable?

I was shocked at her hesitation. In my opinion, there was no question what she should do. She should toss her coffee, pull out her cell phone, call both families and give them the opportunity to help each other.

This is not the time to be politely mum or to expect others to mind their own business.

I'm going to be completely open and honest about 'unacceptable behaviors', a nice way of saying kids who hit their moms. This isn't the time to pussyfoot around the problem and I wouldn't know how if I tried.

"I'm Not Mature Enough"

Are you ready for this? Can you talk about what it's like to get down-and-dirty in hand-to-hand combat with a kid or admit that your child is dominating your life?

Maybe. Maybe you've already *come out of the closet* about it. I respect your courage. You even have friends that know you must practice duck-and-cover on a daily basis. This chapter is going to be great news for you. Maybe it's rated R for some, but to you, it's Disney. I hope you learn something new.

But there are others who aren't so ready. At the mention of physical conflict, you cringe inside. You mentally look away, ready to change the subject.

"Unthinkable! My child could never hurt me. Hitting me? My child? Never!"

You push away the suggestion as though it might be contagious. And yet, reality is that your child hurts you and no one knows. You hide the fear that someday, as your child grows stronger, you will be the only physical barrier to their outbursts. Your reality is destroying you.

A discussion on violence isn't R-rated. It's raw, X-rated footage.

This chapter is for you, too, dear parent.

DEFEND YOURSELF

So how does one get through the day-to-day with a child that doesn't hand out warm fuzzies but often causes pain?

Armor

Arm yourself. Much like the Bible's discussion of the armor of God; the shield of faith, the helmet of salvation and so on, so do we need to find our armor. Arm yourself with understanding, mental filters and realistic expectations. Discover their hot buttons, take responsibility and lose the logic. Have a plan, a strategy. Finally, be prepared to rebuild after battle.

With the armor on, you'll be ready for war.

Understanding

Unlike his mother, Jonathan has an unfailing sense of direction. One day, as we were driving to a convenience store for a treat, I diverted from our normal route. A tennis shoe burst by my right ear, hitting the dash in front of me.

"You're going the wrong way, you're going the wrong way!" Jonathan screamed.

I yelled back, "I'll get us there, don't worry." A tennis ball found its mark on the back of my head while Jonathan kept screaming. Pulling over was impossible so I floored it to the store. Problem solved. Or was it?

Once again I'd survived a *scene*, knowing the next one could be just around the corner. The easy thing to do was saying, "He hates change." The hard part was learning why he hates change.

The battle begins with understanding your child.

With understanding comes confidence and control. Not only do you need it to be that way so that life can become a little more normal, but your child needs it to be that way. Remember, he's counting on you to be in control.

> **Note:** It is possible that your child requires more help. If common sense tells you to fear for you or your family's safety, get professional help immediately. Ask God, your doctor, the school, other mothers for referrals.
>
> You are not the first parent to seek help because your own child is hurting you. Resist the temptation to deny what you're experiencing. It's called pride, which typically precedes even greater pain.

On that drive to the snack store, Jonathan perceived there was a problem. Which meant, there was a problem! He needed to experience resolution as quickly as possible. While another child's brain would have routed the information correctly, telling them, *You can trust your mother*, or even, *You can wait an extra second to see if you'll actually get there*, Jonathan's brain was screaming, *The sky is falling, the sky is falling!*

Depending on your child's condition, you might need to "make it happen" to comfort them. The good news is that as you help their brain to function better (*Children With Starving Brains*, et al.) they will be able to process stress more quickly and efficiently. It does come. But for now, you need to understand their brain's not helping them out.

Use a Mental Filter

I especially love action/adventure movies. My heart races and I start shivering in my seat. I'm sure I delivered my first child two weeks early because of *The Terminator.*

Over the years, I've developed my own technique for handling excitement and still enjoy the movie. When the music starts to build and I can tell the proverbial ax is about to fall, I hold my hand to my face, spreading my fingers ever so slightly until I can barely see the screen. I filter the impact to the degree that I need, and when I feel the tension ease, I lower my hand.

Maybe this would be a good time for you to do just that: employ a filtering element.

Take in information at your own pace. (This is not meant to justify coming to a full stop.) Remind yourself that no one faces this subject without fear and dread.

Find a filter that will relieve the stress. Laughter's a great filter. So are mental breaks like keeping a journal, writing a letter to God, or going to Target for popcorn. Find someone to talk to. Apply your own mental filter to enable yourself to learn as much as you can about this subject.

Accept Responsibility

Every time I tell my little girl to get dressed for school she whines.

"Comb your hair," I say and she whimpers pathetically. I tell her to go brush her teeth and she moans, "I can't do it by myself". I tell her to clean up her room and she uses her most pitiful voice, saying, "I need help". We go back and forth until she has two minutes to brush her teeth, comb her hair and pick up her room.

At which time I look her in the eye and say, "Fine, you'll be getting in the car in your pajamas and there will be no TV the rest of the week."

In ninety seconds, she's in the car, dressed and ready to go.

I'm trying to teach my daughter that *she's* responsible for her actions, or lack thereof, and trust we'll eventually get there.

I wish there was someone else in charge. But there's not. This one is all yours. Throughout this laborious, often painful process of working with a different child, accept the fact that you're in the driver's seat.

It would be so easy to send a child off to an all-day program, then set them in front of a computer screen to keep them busy until bedtime, all while pretending your life is normal.

You are your child's greatest advocate. If positive things aren't happening, goals being set, objectives being met, or learning going on, *someone's* dropped the ball.

Accept the challenge that it's your responsibility to keep everyone on the same page. Question teachers about how you can work together on a problem. Be creative in exposing your child to challenges like greater responsibilities at home or school.

Accepting responsibility also means being ready to respond. Not to react, but to *respond*. One is in control, the other isn't.

When Jonathan had an outburst, *reacting* meant spitting and hissing like an angry cat. *Responding* meant holding him the way I'd been taught, waiting for him to process the information, and sticking with the appropriate consequence. Responding showed Jonathan I loved him and he didn't have to be afraid that I was going to lose control. He could see my confidence and be secure in the fact that I knew what to do (even though I didn't always feel that way).

Accepting responsibility might have another beneficial effect. You might begin to realize that your child is also responsible for their actions, and suddenly you find yourself feeling less sorry for them. It's wonderful.

Realistic Expectations

When the State Fair came to town, I thought it would be great for Jonathan and I to go together, so off we went.

We arrived just as the gates opened. Unknown to me, Jonathan had his mind set on one ride and one ride only. That particular ride wasn't scheduled to open for an hour. Because I hadn't researched the times, nor talked with Jonathan about what to expect, he exploded. He was furious with the unopened ride and with me. Within ten minutes, after purchasing two tickets and paying ten dollars for parking, we were back in the car and on our way home. I was furious and told him so.

To be honest, my expectations were way off. I expected him to handle the stimulating environment, disappointment and change, all at once. I had to remind myself that Jonathan is not like most ten-year-olds. I'd thrown too much at him.

I don't expect Jonathan to handle every circumstance, or to listen up (!) or logically process my list of reasons why he shouldn't be upset. I understand that he needs to be prepared for a situation and given some discussion about what we'll be doing or not doing. It's my job to have realistic expectations.

Avoid Stress Where You Can

Learn your child's hot buttons. What causes stress for them?

Crowds? Loud noises? Toy stores? Birthday parties, where presents are only for the birthday boy, balloons are popping, and only one kid is supposed to blow out the candles? I went to all those parties and took Jonathan to the loud and crowded places. He needed to learn how to cope, I reasoned. Wrong. All it did was upset us both.

This is your permission to say "no" to the things that add stress to your day.

Now that you've got your defenses in order, it's time to prepare an offense.

CHAPTER EIGHT

Let's Get Physical: Offense

PART II

WHAT'S YOUR PLAN?

During those first battles, Jonathan was counting on me to stay in my corner while he threw from his. If he was hitting me, I stayed passive, all while he made contact; fists pounding, biting, and kicking. "What plan?" I would have said, "I have no plan!"

Now is the time to formulate a plan, an *offense*.

ARSENAL

Just as you need armor for a good defense, it's critical to know what makes up a good offense. I recommend an arsenal of strategic weapons.

Be Prepared

Learn to recognize signs that your child is about to lose control. The second you see aggression, move immediately toward him and take his wrists in a strong hold. He can't throw things if you're in his face and you'll be prepared to restrain his whole body if you need to. It also gives the impression that you are in control.

Choose Your Ground

Have a place picked out for your child when they're out of control. *The key in this offensive element is speed and determination.*

At first, I handled Jonathan wherever the meltdown occurred. But that meant my room, the living room, the dining room (all dangerous places to be out of control). I decided on his room. Quickly herding Jonathan to his room kept him off balance and unable to hurt me. Later, when Jonathan was able to control himself, just the warning of "Do I need to hold you?" or, "Let's go to your room," was the incentive he needed to calm down.

Learn How to Hold

You're child is out of control. His processing abilities have shut down. He's already shifted to autopilot. He's scared. He needs your help to get back into control.

Holding is an effective way to keep the child from hurting himself, you and others. It provides a safe environment, down time for his brain to process through the stress, and a safe way to help him regain control and his dignity.

Note: For some children, slow, deep muscle pressure slows down those rapid-firing brains and helps them think.

When Jonathan is reaching a certain level of stress, we often stop for a 'push and pull'. While facing each other, he lies down on his back and puts his feet to my shoulders. I alternately let him push his feet into my shoulders, and then pull his legs toward me, stretching him as much as I can. He feels the stretch/pressure in the large muscles of his arms and legs. In a matter of minutes, he is calm again.

It's All in the Wrist

Use your body weight to hold the child still. Slowly "force" them to the floor, the bed, rug, etc. Try to apply pressure while not constricting. *You do not want to hurt them*, you want to immobilize them, so that they can't hurt you or themselves. At the same time, your pressure reassures them that you are in control, which, in turn, helps *them* regain control of their bodies.

Control the arms by holding both wrists. *Important: Whether they are on their stomachs or backs, keep your face away from their head. Or, use your arm as a buffer between the two. One good head butt can break a nose or cheekbone.*

Use your legs to control their legs.

Now you wait.

Still Holding: Your Face

A very wise teacher once told me that a child's greatest fear is an adult out of control.

You are going to be very emotional through this scene. Zoe probably broke the hand-painted plate left to you by a favorite relative, or a knife went whizzing by your left ear. You've never been angrier. Feelings of hysteria, betrayal and revenge are running through your mind.

You're about to play the greatest role of your life.

Show no emotion.

Be silent or speak in a quiet monotone. Don't show anger, fear, confusion, or frustration. Not one knitted brow. Even if this child has never caught a social cue before in his life, he will catch your emotional feedback immediately, so lose the expressions.

This is one of the hardest habits to learn. All parents have a patented *look* to give their normal kids. But give one in a stressful moment and the different child moves with hyper-speed into an off-the-chart meltdown.

Learn the rules your child lives by, the ones his brain *makes* him live by.

Still Holding

Tone of Voice. Just as important is the tone of your voice. It must be calm and controlled. No matter how mad you are, even through your tears, you need to provide a blank page to help your child regain composure.

The fewer the words, the better. Silence is best. Their brains aren't processing anything at this point and your words, just like your expression, will only increase the jumble inside their brains.

Reduce *all* sensory input. Cut down on what they have to process. Turn off the radio or TV, avoid eye contact, keep your voice calm and turn out lights if possible.

Provide structure. One day at school, I watched Jonathan's teacher handle a tantrum. He was screaming about something and when asked to stop, he threw a chair. She immediately guided Jonathan into the hall, where two little chairs waited. He picked up one and threw it, then dropped into the other. Instead of reacting, she knelt down, staring at the floor, removing all stimuli from herself to Jonathan. After a quiet second, she began to speak but Jonathan interrupted her with angry screams. Again, she went silent. As soon as he was quiet again, she said, "Jonathan, I'll wait for you to stop screaming." He yelled. She calmly repeated the words, "Jonathan, I'm waiting for you to calm down," and, "I can't talk to you while you're screaming." Finally, he realized she really would wait as long as it took for him to get in control of his voice. Soon, he calmed down and they discussed the problem.

Remember, you are in charge. You must provide the structure. The place, the words, and the holding all must be consistent.

Still Holding but Over the Struggle

Once They're Calm - You're on top of your child. Eventually, the rhythm of their breath slows. They become quiet. Slowly relax your hold. Using the same words every time, ask, "Jonathan, are you in control?" The answer determines whether or not you can begin to release your hold.

Stop Holding - Only immobilize while they can't think (process language, stress, etc.). You are doing them a favor. Once they've begun to process again, it's time to release the hold and begin to communicate.

Recovery

Now it's time to process what happened. Be patient. This is transitional time. You know they're ready when they can communicate, though they might want time alone before talking about it.

Continue to stay in control of your emotions. *Slowly*, reintroduce stimuli (eye contact, movement, words). Keep your voice soothing and use very few words. Use short, simple phrases. If the tantrum launched "for no good reason", don't try to convince your child he was being unreasonable. Their brain has determined that they must react. Personally, I chose a comforting role at this time.

The ideal is for the child to take responsibility for their actions, though this varies with every child.

Deal with the Truth

After a few minutes to restore the relationship, find the consistent words appropriate to your child's understanding to explain the bad behavior and use that exact same phrase every time.

"Throwing hurts."

"Kicking is not okay."

"When you bite, you are making a bad choice."

There may or may not be remorse. This is an exercise in appropriate responses. The goal is their acceptance of responsibility, but until you get there, go through the motions. Have your consequences in place and stick to them.

Consequences

You are reading the confessions of a once die-hard believer in my son's inability to deal with stress, accept responsibility or to suffer consequences. It took a wake-up call from Jonathan's teachers to learn otherwise. There must be consequences, which are addressed more thoroughly in Chapter Nine.

Restore the Relationship

Find the sweet moments. I always told Jonathan I loved him after an episode. I would always hug him. Often, we cried. Sometimes, I had to talk about what certain things meant to me or how sad I was he'd broken them, or how much he'd hurt me. I'm not sure that was the right thing to do, but the hug always helped.

I hope this chapter has given you a better handle on physical confrontation. And, in case there's any doubt, imagine your darkest hour and hear me when I say, it's going to get better. You aren't the first or only one in that dark place, so keep searching, treating, and hoping.

I leave you here with great news. Someday, this subject might also be your past and despite any pride or fear of meddling, you will also be driven to help others handle the same.

CHAPTER NINE

The Three C'S

Parents of normal children, particularly of the firstborn, have tiny measuring sticks all around them. Their normal child is in a play group, church group, or mother's day out program, all with a roomful of kids to tell them what developmental stage their child should be at. They *see* what to expect.

Parents of different children don't have those little barometers of behaviors to learn from. We are so busy struggling to understand where in the heck we are, that we often stop moving ahead.

Looking back, I wish I'd had a class in Different Childhood Development 101. Instead, here are three subjects of interest that might help you judge where your child is and where they should be.

CHANGING EXPECTATIONS

I was referred to a mother whose son, I was told, *used to be just like Jonathan.*

I knew this boy. *Like Jonathan? Impossible.* This young man, six years older, was sociable, enjoyed doing different things and had virtually no behavioral problems.

Despite my track record, I do hate learning the hard way, so I asked this woman a simple question.

"What would you have done differently?"

Immediately, she said, "I would have expected a whole lot more, a lot more sooner."

"Hmmm," I nodded, scratching my chin, wondering what in the heck she meant.

TRAINED PARENT

By the time Jonathan was six, I had become a well-trained parent. I was trained to avoid crowds and to expect screams and hitting. I was convinced that he couldn't wait to be satisfied and therefore, could justify any outburst over any thing that displeased him. I became a student of scenarios that could upset his little brain, avoiding them like the plague.

It's all about survival, right? Not really. It took a Come-to-Jesus meeting at the school to help me see the light.

Houston, We Have a Problem

We started having a little problem called, "I'm not going to school without kicking and screaming." Jonathan would fight me into the car, open the door while it was moving, try to grab the steering wheel, etc. About that time, I reached my physical limit and began relying on two teachers from the school to come and pick him up.

Something's wrong at school, I decided. *It must be the teachers or what they're teaching.* We spent weeks trying to figure it out, with no insight. I was as frustrated as the school.

Then, one day, we called a meeting. The principal, two teachers, and the school counselor. I was in store for a rude awakening.

"The window of opportunity is closing, Diane," they said. "Things have got to change at home. Jonathan is getting too big to be fighting you like this. He's not going to be able to hold down a job and you won't be able to take him anywhere."

At home? (That's the only part I heard.) *What at home? This meeting wasn't about me, was it? Surely not.*

"Jonathan is getting away with too much," they said.

"But he's good at home," I told them. "He goes from the computer to the trampoline, to the TV, or just spends time in his room. He never gives me trouble. Except when I ask him to do something he doesn't want to do, of course."

"Of course he's not going to want to come to school if he gets to do whatever he wants to at home," they said, stating the obvious.

"So what am I supposed to do?" I asked defensively.

Their answer was firm. Take charge. Ask him to do things he doesn't want to do but most importantly, give him consequences for bad behavior.

"At home?"

"Especially at home."

I left that meeting feeling doomed. I'd survived the physical confrontations and learned how to avoid them. Now they were asking me to do things that I knew would bring it all back. Just the thought of those bad memories made me weep.

I could only pray for supernatural strength and prepare to face the behaviors I knew would come.

Manipulation

I think it's no coincidence when something else happened that same week to help me expect more of Jonathan. This time, it was of my husband's doing.

Jonathan's passion was computer games, and he craved new ones regularly. We tried to justify his passion by only buying the 'educational' ones, but we were still buying them often.

The week of the school meeting, Jonathan asked for a new game. My husband was in the room and immediately told him he *might* get it at the end of the week. It was Tuesday. Jonathan began to scream.

"If you scream, no TV all week and no video game on Friday," my husband said calmly.

Great, I thought, *now I'm the one who's going to have to live with the screaming. Of course he can't control himself for a week! Poor baby.*

For one week, the *poor baby* was a perfect angel. Not one tantrum, whine or plea.

I may be slow but I'm not stupid. I'd been manipulated for the last time. He understood perfectly what it took to get that game and he did it.

Laying down the law suddenly became a lot easier.

Changing Expectations

The new laws were very simple.

'Be in the car by 8:15 am, or no privileges the rest of the day (TV or computer).'

'You hit, you lose your privileges.'

'You scream at Mom, you lose your privileges.'

It took two days for Jonathan to get it and in over two years, we've had a problem getting to school once.

Changing expectations means no matter where your child is developmentally, keep raising the bar. You know they're not like Jimmy and Sally at the daycare, but that's not your measuring stick. From where you are, raise the bar.

BUT FIRST,

Eliminate the Physical

By the time I was ready to expect more of Jonathan, we'd cleaned up his diet and a chronic yeast infection. We'd also been supplying the nutrients that his brain needed (and was now able to absorb). I felt comfortable expecting more of Jonathan because his health was not going to inhibit his ability to control himself. We just had a lot of bad habits to break.

Stop Feeling Sorry for Them

I suddenly realized how sorry I'd been feeling for Jonathan. So sorry, in fact, that I felt like he never *deserved* any consequences. He had so few interests, I felt guilty at the thought of taking those things away.

You've heard many times of disabled young children and their parents who treat them as 'normal'. To do otherwise is crippling. But when it's your own child, and you've grown up with the difficulties, it's not easy.

Stop helping/protecting your child so much that no one knows what they're capable of. Only by raising the bar of expectations can they reach their full potential.

Picture Goals

Do you want your child to be able to function in society? Do you want them to be able to do things they don't like? What are you working toward?

According to the experts, an infant is ready to eat Cheerios when their fingers are mature (coordinated) enough to pick them up. Our kids are the same.

Are they tall enough to reach the sink? If so, they can help with the dishes. Are they strong enough to open drawers to put away clothes? They certainly have the time.

You will see an increase in self-esteem and pride as they successfully accomplish goals you've set. On the other hand, expecting nothing will only isolate, and cause resentment, between them and their siblings.

Have break-time goals. With summer and holiday breaks, the child is faced with a lack of structure. As parents, we have more time to help on a regular basis.

Our summer goals have included learning to tie shoes, fold clothes, take out the garbage, etc. Do they collect something? Start an allowance and make it their responsibility to pay for what they want. Give them a chance to earn money.

Changing expectations is where you must begin. Only after you believe your child can be successful, can you enforce a consequence if they fail.

Consider what you expect of your child, right now, and ask yourself, is that enough? Are you willing to change your thinking so that your child may prove to you they can be so much more?

CONSEQUENCES

Everyone Qualifies

"No discipline seems pleasant at the time, but painful. Later on, however, it produces a harvest of righteousness and peace for those

who have been trained by it." Hebrews 12:11, New International Version.

When my kids complain about my parenting skills, which they do regularly, I generally fall back on a reliable explanation. "God made me your mother. If you've got a problem with that, take it up with Him."

It's our job, as parents, to allow our kids to suffer the consequences, now or later. If it's now, they're generally still safe at home, under your watchful eye. If it's later, it could be a correctional facility or a hospital.

With a different child, I know it's much harder to enforce consequences. Looking back, having learned the hard way, I have a few ideas about how to save yourself some grief.

Start Early

It all boils down to what you will put up with. If you wait until the child is four to expect self-control, they'll gladly meet your expectations. Not until five? Be my guest. Two? You're laying the foundation for a well-behaved kid.

I think if I had it to do over again, and the second Jonathan started throwing a tantrum over my decisions, I'd hold him. Every time he'd start to scream, I'd remove what he was playing with. At the same time, I'd reward the good behavior with something he liked. I'd show him as early as possible that he would be pleased with good choices and denied something with his bad choices. I'd try harder at being consistent early on.

I wouldn't leave the house without a plan, and always preface the outing with, "Now, if you decide to (misbehave), there will be this consequence. But if you are…, there is a reward.

Note: I believe that many of Jonathan's behaviors were physiologically related, which we eventually dealt with. However, I still would have expected more.

Give Choices

They want red. You offer them green or blue. They want candy. You offer them fruit or crackers. They want to watch an hour-long show, you agree to thirty minutes. There's a fine line between proving who's in charge, and helping them avoid feeling stressed out.

Re-Direct

Nothing new to parents, re-directing is a way of helping the different child handle stress. The pressure is building toward something they want, or don't want, to do. You draw their attention to something else and the gun never goes off.

There are other inherent talents in learning how to re-direct.

Sometimes, it's necessary to forget the rules. In a situation where other people are having to suffer the consequences of a child's bad behavior, I think it's okay to do what's necessary to avoid the confrontation. For example, you're at the airport. They want another cookie. You say no, they start to scream. This might not be the best time to tell them they're about to lose all their privileges or sit in time out. As with any rule, there's always going to be the exception.

Sometimes, it's necessary to deceive. You're in a very quiet library and an explosion is imminent because you didn't check out the right book. That's when you say, "Oh, I forgot, I already got that book and it's at home," or "the librarian wants us to come back tomorrow for it." An immediate feeling of hope takes care of the conflict. This allows you to pick the *where* your child must handle his stress.

Be Flexible

Still, with consequences, there are certain situations in which I think the expectations should change. For example, the baby-sitter shouldn't have to be responsible for enforcing a strict level of restrictions. Make it a treat to have a baby-sitter and allow extra TV time, to have desert if they behave, etc. A four-day weekend? Loosen up a little. Has the day been extra stressful? Offer extra computer time so that you can relax.

The A-B-C Level of Infractions

This simple way of rating consequences has helped me not sweat the small stuff.

Level A - The most serious consequences involve safety, like wearing a seatbelt, lying, hitting (causing harm to himself or others). This warrants severe consequences.

Level B - Developmental expectations such as respect, using words instead of screaming, blatant disobedience. Give a warning, choices, and consequences.

Level C - Minor infractions such as arguing with siblings (try to let them work it out), forgetting his chores. Not conscious disobedience. Handle quickly and forget about it.

As always, be open to underlying causes. These may include sensory issues (need to chew), tired, needs movement, headaches, low blood sugar (needs some protein), etc.

CONSEQUENCES FOR YOU

Responsibility

Consequences help teach responsibility. If a child is obviously motivated to do their job, whether it's putting dishes in the sink or getting dressed in the morning without whining, they are learning to be self-reliant.

Again, they must be allowed to suffer the consequences when they fail. You allow them to find out what it's like to not have enough money when it's time to go to the store, or if they've forgotten their homework, they can't watch TV. It's all about enforcing consequences.

Self-Control

Knowing there are consequences, give privileges with limits they can learn to enforce themselves. "At 2:00, you may have a snack," or, "when the timer goes off, turn off the TV." Perhaps your child is able to get his own snacks and/or fix his own lunch. He chooses from what he knows is allowed, and asks when he's got another idea. The help is great, and it gives him independence as well as a chance to practice self-control.

As always, lavish the praise when they succeed, and have a consequence when they don't.

Respect

The beauty of consequences is that they can be used to instill the practice of respect in *all* children. It is a learned behavior for everyone, but sometimes we forget our different kids can learn it, too. Language, facial expressions, tone of voice (this is a biggie in my house), behaviors, etc., all reflect respect to the parent, peers, siblings and themselves. Work towards expecting respect with a consequence for the lack of.

Use the word *respect* when you talk about expectations and conse-quences. "You are being disrespectful when you...," and still, apply the con-sequences. When Jonathan slammed a door so hard he put a dent in it, I made him empty his wallet, everything he had, to help pay for it.

Respect means learning how to resolve conflict. It's learning how to respect people and their property. Respect means using words, not fists. It also means that you, the parent, will listen, listen, listen.

COMPROMISE

The third "C" is *Compromise*, although a better word might be *flexibility*. It means being able to deal with situations, moment by moment, taking in all the variables, and applying reasonable judgment.

For example, you're at a store that has video games for customers to try out. Clarence starts to play. You want to leave. Instead of demanding the child stop immediately, you compromise. "You may play five more minutes, then turn it off." If they argue, "then we need to leave now."

You go out to eat and hope Zoe can stay at the table for an hour. Sitting at a table, with, in her mind, nothing to do, is not 'safe'. It's much better to take along something that is safe for her (a favorite game, book, toy) that she gets to play after eating her meal and sitting quietly at the table for fifteen minutes.

Ask yourself, *Is it Reasonable*? Because I know my son's strengths and weaknesses, I evaluate his behavior differently than that of my other children. If he makes an unusual request that would normally elicit a "no," I try to evaluate the circumstances. Is he verbalizing his needs appropriately? Does he have reasons why he should be allowed a positive response? Has he shown self-control? Has he done what I asked? If those things apply, I often say, "yes".

The key is balance. As often as I say *Yes*, I need to say *No*, giving my child a chance to practice delayed gratification. "You may have it tomorrow," and "Save your money until Friday," or, "If you brush your teeth every day this week, we'll get that." We all need practice handling *No*.

Challenge your child beginning today. Wherever he is on the developmental scale, because he needs your help to move to the next level, keep raising the bar of expectations while having predictable, consistent consequences. In the end, you will provide your child with a growing sense of accomplishment, independence, and an ability to make good choices.

CHAPTER TEN

The *Different* Family

Just in time for my firstborn, *What to Expect When You're Expecting* hit bookstores everywhere. It was like the pregnant woman's Bible. Today, there's a whole slew of *What to Expect* books, and writers everywhere are wishing they'd thought of it first. The public's appetite for learning what *not* to do is insatiable.

So where was that *What to Expect for Families When You Have a Different Child* book? Even I, the expert in *avoidance*, was starving for advice on how to help my normal children.

I needed help and I needed it yesterday!

WHAT TO EXPECT

If you knew that over time raising a different child would have a significant impact on your social and emotional ability to function as a parent; that problems such as depression, fear and anxiety, difficulties in daily management of the child, burnout, financial worries, and concerns over adequate educational and professional resources would arise; would you have done something different for the child and for your family?

That's the question I asked parents and siblings of grown children with physical disabilities, Asperger's syndrome, autism and bi-polar disorder.

THE EXPERTS

The presence of a different child profoundly affects the whole family. Every individual and every relationship, between husband and wife, between parent and normal child, and among siblings themselves, is impacted. It affects how your neighbors treat you, if friends call you, and how the clerk at the grocery store looks at you.

Parents often find themselves buried under an emotional pile, too busy or empty to head off isolation and depression. They forget to nurture other siblings waiting in the wings.

Handling a different child can be a terrific problem, because no one prepares you for it. Sadly, only in the midst of it all, do you acknowledge that you're doing it wrong, and yet, there's no one to tell you how to do it right.

Just like those *What to Expect* books, I feel there is value in hearing what the experts (those who have raised a different child) have to say. Though everyone's story is different, there's something comforting in hearing what struggles were met, head on, and endured. I hope you find a *take-with*.

WHAT DO THE EXPERTS SAY

Parents and children were asked to discuss their struggles in regard to their different child or sibling. They were asked what they would have done differently (or wish their parents had done differently), what struggles they experienced and what they learned to accept. This is an honest recording of their struggles. Editing was kept to a minimum and names have been changed.

Claire - son, Roger (20), autism, daughter, Rayna.

When both were small, I had to spend so much time watching Roger, Rayna perceived that I loved him more. We talked a lot about how much I loved her, and she eventually understood that.

I tried to find the humor in the tense moments. Rayna and I would team up and agree to ignore Roger's bad behaviors when they were obviously done for attention. She was a great partner.

We were never able to go on vacations or out to eat.

I regret that Rayna couldn't have friends over and we never went to other's homes as a family. It isolated her. I tried to help her develop friendships, sometimes calling other moms to have Rayna over, but it was never enough.

I had to fight so hard for Roger against the public school district, I kept Rayna at a private school and tried to participate there while Roger was in school. I didn't have the energy to address Rayna's learning differences because they were so insignificant compared to Roger's. I knew she'd get by.

Because of our finances, we weren't able to have help or to get away. There's really nothing I could have done differently because of our finances.

Rayna, by personality and because of her brother, was deeply compassionate and sensitive. She had a seed of kindness that is rare. She was completely non-judgmental and accepting of others.

Linda - son, Chris (15), mild ASD, 3 other children

I had four kids, five and under. Chris, the second oldest, had to go with the flow. Sometimes that meant leaving a grocery store or park, but I had to take him with me, everywhere we went. I expected him to behave. We were quick with the consequences when he didn't. In public, I wasn't embarrassed. His siblings responded to that. Today, when his siblings bring home a friend, it's understood. They're accepting of Chris or they're not welcome.

A lot comes with maturity, at least for siblings.

Mary - younger sister, Leslie (40's), epilepsy, severe panic disorder, partial paralysis

My parents were quick to squash my accomplishments because it wasn't right that I outshine Leslie. There were always mixed messages - 'you can do anything but don't excel to make Leslie feel bad.'

My parents lived on the edge of a crisis.

I remember being angry because my parents didn't investigate her panic disorder. We just lived with it. There was this constant conflict between loving my sister and needing to protect her, and the resentment that I was supposed to love her and take care of her.

My parents never talked to me about my sister's differences. I never had a chance to express my fear or embarrassment, which, at times made me very angry. I remember feeling guilty because 'I'm okay and Leslie's not'. We were supposed to feel sorry for her, yet she could do anything I could do.

I felt humiliated during Leslie's very public panic attacks.

Leslie clung to me for safety all through school. I was very protective of Leslie.

I wish my parents had verbalized their appreciation of my help, talked about the situation, asked me, 'what do you need?' or 'what would have helped?'

It has taken years in to adulthood for the dynamics to change between us. As the protective older sister, it took a long time to be able to be vulnerable with Leslie. Now we have a wonderful relationship.

Gina – son, Michael (18), bi-polar

I wish I'd recognized that there was something I could do for Michael a lot sooner. Getting a call from the high school telling me my son was mentally ill was one of the worst days of my life. I had no idea he needed that kind of help. I felt so alone, that no one else could possibly understand. I wish I'd found a support group a lot sooner.

Every other week, I tried to take Michael and a friend somewhere to help him socially.

Michael is brilliant (began reading at three) but can barely get it on paper for passing grades. Still, I tell Michael to be proud of who he is and to hold his head high.

Prayer and knowing God is the only thing that got us through, and my relationship with Him now is body, soul and spirit. Praise God!

I would tell other parents to seek help and not allow the stigma of mental illness to stop you.

Michael is a brilliant kid, who has learned to manage his anger (by being held responsible for his actions) but will always be an organizational mess.

David (13) - younger brother, Steven (11), autism

I still feel embarrassed by my brother. I wish I'd gotten to do a lot more stuff without him being around to embarrass me. I feel sorry for Steven, and sorry that I've missed out on going to places because of the chance of being embarrassed.

I love Steven. I try to understand why more is expected of me.

Michelle – brother, Matt (30's), suspected Asperger's syndrome

My parents tried and tried to find out what was different about my brother. The doctors finally said he had minor brain damage from birth. Only recently, Matt's in his late thirties, have they suspected Asperger's syndrome.

Matt lives with my parents, works and seems happy. I feel guilty that he has no friends or social life. Matt has a good job, he drives and takes care of himself though he still lives with my parents. They are pretty much his only company.

I have to work at not feeling guilty that I don't include him in my family's activities, but I can't do that to my husband. I know the day will come when my parents are gone and I'll be the one to keep an eye on Matt. He'll be fine living by himself but I'll make sure it's close by.

Sharon – son, Chris (20) with Asperger's syndrome, daughter (18)

Chris was considered severely autistic (with savant characteristics) when he was little. Now, at twenty, he's finished two years of Junior College and is enrolled at a university for the Fall.

Chris was very tactilely defensive as a child, so there wasn't a lot we could do until he was ready. But things like sensory integration, speech therapy, occupational therapy and horseback riding helped tremendously.

> I wish I'd worked harder at developing relationships with others who could be his friends as he got older. The kids at school knew him and were always nice, but college is a different story. No one knows him and he'd like to have friends.

The Author - son, Jonathan (11), Asperger's Syndrome

I often called my husband at work when things got bad. It helped that he could come home to help. I'd crater more easily than him when our son tantrumed in public, so generally he took charge while I hung with the rest of the family.

I wish I'd asked for help at church a lot sooner, just so my husband and I could have a couple of hours together. I wish I'd gone on the Internet a lot sooner to find support groups, doctors and therapies.

I would have *died* (my word) unless I'd seen the goodness of the Lord in the land of the living. (Psalm 27:13)

WHAT'S NORMAL

Among the siblings of the families I talked with, certain feelings, good and bad, appeared to be universal.

Isolation

Embarrassment

Sensitivity

Emotional Discernment

Resentment (particularly among siblings)

Stages of Mourning, Anger and Acceptance

How Parents Can Help

Parents, accept imperfections in all your children. It's important that husband and wife act as a team, and you can't if you don't agree/admit there's a problem.

Be sensitive to each other's feelings and practice taking turns allowing the other to be 'stressed out'.

Watch for opportunities to be alone with each child. Focus on that child. Spend *some* time talking and listening. Give them the tools to understand, make sure they know that you understand their feelings and love them.

Enlist the help of teachers, family and friends. I can't emphasize enough the monumental importance of asking for help. In every discussion with families, I heard over and over, "I felt so isolated." Ignore the feelings of embarrassment, doubt and fear and tell people that you need help.

3 Wishes For The Rest Of The Family

Talk and Listen. I don't believe it's possible to eliminate the difficult circumstances listed above. However, the ability to talk and listen seems to instill in normal children a maturity well beyond their years.

Getting away from the stress is critical. Your family responds to your stress. Also, you are sacrificing your own health if you don't.

Finding a support group is critical. It is a wish of every experienced parent that this had happened sooner. You will find occasion to laugh and learn about the latest in solutions.

CHAPTER ELEVEN

Jonathan's Story

Jonathan, our second child, was a perfect baby. A ten on the Apgar Scale. He laughed, he babbled, he sat up and slept well. Only in language (at about eighteen months) did we notice a delay. He was not putting words together at the appropriate milestones.

But nothing seemed serious. He loved numbers, counting to fifty before three. He loved words and we realized he could read before his fourth birthday. But the preference to play by himself, inattention to us when we spoke to him, and the language delay got our attention.

When Jonathan was three, we began testing: hearing tests, a developmental pediatrician, a pediatric neurologist and eventually with the school system. The developmental pediatrician told us Jonathan was probably PDD/NOS: Pervasive Developmental Disorder/Not Otherwise Specified. Her suggestion was to continue speech therapy and to enter an early childhood program through the school, though any structured program would be helpful.

Jonathan's violent behaviors increased significantly during that time. He was hitting, head-butting, biting, and screaming louder than you can imagine. All my experience as a mother flew out the window. Nothing seemed to work and my life began to revolve around this unpredictable tornado.

During this time, my husband brought home reams of 'chat' material he'd found on the Internet. It was a web site of moms discussing the link between diet and behavior. My first thought was, "Well, Jonathan doesn't eat much sugar, he's not hyper, so it doesn't concern me."

"No, no, no," my husband said, "they're talking about the effects of dairy products on these kids. I think you should look at it."

"I don't think so," was the gist of my response and the reams of paper ended up in the trash, along with several good books he'd given me.

Between ages four and six is a blur. It was a dark time. We tested Jonathan's hearing again, still with no problems. He was receiving speech therapy and in-home play therapy provided by the school system, which taught me how to encourage language.

We also tried homeopathic remedies combined with an exercise therapy. However, the chaos at home made attempting this mode of treatment one more nightmare and we gave up.

We were introduced to sensory integration therapy during this time. This helped significantly as Jonathan was able to relax using the deep muscle techniques they encouraged. He was able to stay in control for longer periods of time and his school work benefited. Speech therapy continued.

Two years later, I was seated next to a woman at our children's swimming lesson. Her oldest and my oldest were in the same group, the only boys in a class of ten. We made a few jokes, started talking, and Jonathan, taking a private lesson off to the side, caught her attention.

"My son used to be a lot like that."

"Oh no, your son is nowhere close to being like mine," I said, watching her son swim and interact in the older class.

She began to describe to me the $2,000/month worth of therapy she'd been doing with him and his special school. Recently, she'd read about how diet affects certain kids. She'd started a gluten and casein-free diet and within a couple of weeks, every therapist was sure she'd changed medications, upped medications or flat out said she didn't need to come any more.

It was my first introduction to the gluten-free/casein-free diet. Still, I bristled at the perceived effort.

Then she said, "The nice thing is, you can test their urine and see if the diet will help."

I could do that!

The tests (Great Plains Laboratory, OAT and Peptide tests) showed Jonathan had a chronic (undetected for several years) yeast infection and was not digesting the gluten (grains) and casein (dairy) in his diet. It was the motivation I needed to devote my time and attention to learning what to do. In retrospect, changing my kitchen around was a breeze compared to handling the tantrums.

Removing wheat and dairy gave us immediate results. The tantrums almost completely evaporated.

At this time, I attended a DAN! Conference (Defeat Autism Now) and learned of several commonalities for children with ASD including a poor immune system, zinc deficiency, and calcium and essential fatty acid deficiencies, all needed by the brain to function normally.

Rather than order and wait on more test results, I called up Kirkman Labs and ordered one of each supplement recommended. Based on Jonathan's behaviors, I already knew his brain needed help. It was too easy to start giving him the different supplements and watch for improvement.

It was unbelievable. Within a couple of weeks, Jonathan's logic, reasoning, language, sense of humor, and more, kicked in to high gear. We gave him a superior pro-biotic called Essential Formulas and the yeast infection disappeared. This resulted in consistent formed bowel movements and immediately no more diapers.

Along with the probiotic, we gave Jonathan colostrum (also from Kirkman Labs). That was the last time Jonathan got sick. No more yearly upper respiratory infections, no more flu (the whole family takes it instead of getting the flu shot) and there was a significant decrease in allergies.

After a year on the strict gluten-free/casein-free diet, (and also two years of taking L-glutamin, a gut-healer), it was my decision to begin giving him enzymes from Houston Neutraceuticals (Houstonni.com) whenever he ate wheat or dairy. In our case, Jonathan's behavior improved even more and it was a blessing to forgo the diet.

At nine, Jonathan no longer reacted to gluten and casein and we discontinued the enzymes.

Between ages eight and ten, we watched Jonathan's gradual improvement. We began seeing a DAN doctor and tried secretin shots and glutathione shots. They helped some. After three shots, we discontinued them.

During this time, we decided to begin chelation (removal of mercury) knowing all of Jonathan's vaccinations had included mercury. We began with DMSA, added ALA, and, because Jonathan's body/immune system were so strong by this time, we never had any problem with yeast or gut bugs, as many do. We added daily alithiamine and glutathione creams as well. After nine months, we were seeing only tiny bits of mercury.

Zinc is a natural chelator and we'd been giving Jonathan a good amount for several years by then. That might be why we saw so little mercury. Anyway, we decided to stop the chelation. The creams smelled and we were tired.

THIS LAST YEAR

At ten, Jonathan is doing great. He is still uninterested in pursuing friendships, though he plays well with family members. His language is lacking in pragmatics. Though advanced in vocabulary, his words don't flow naturally and his choice of words is odd, though, if we ask him to slow down or repeat the question, his words are fine. Handling stress is only occasionally an issue.

Neurofeedback

I learned about a therapist in my area doing some great things for people with neurological disorders using a specific type of neurofeedback she developed called Sweet Spot Training. She likens it to finding the sweet spot on a bat, looking for the specific spots in the brain that are either under- or over-stimulated, and helping them become balanced, i.e., a gym for the brain.

I read *Symphony of the Brain* and was fascinated. It seemed logical to me that stimulating certain areas of the brain could help.

After forty sessions, Jonathan no longer flaps his hands (though he occasionally focuses on his fingers when excited) and the sensory part of his brain has literally awakened.

His independence has soared. He's become more goal-oriented—earning money for a game or thinking about a summer vacation. His math skills have improved (word problems particularly) and his ability to handle stress has improved even more. We've had several conversations he's initiated to work through our disagreements.

We plan on allowing Jonathan's brain to settle in to these new behaviors, then do a few more sessions of Sweet Spot Training in the near future.

Finally, I was reading the book *Treating Autism: Parent Stories of Hope and Success* and a mother's story about her successful use of homeopathy caught my attention. I have contacted a specialist who has treated children with ASD and we are going to eventually pursue.

Am I looking for perfection? The magic bullet? The cure? No. But I am looking for things that might help his body. As long as Jonathan needs help, as with my other children, I'm going to remain watchful. The point is that I believe many things about the human body are treatable. Not everything is fixable. But until something inside of me says "Done", I'm going to stay vigilant. Who knows how this story ends.

A Letter to Moms

I stopped going for perfect a long time ago.

Somewhere between Kansas and Oz, I lost the notion that hope and happiness and normalcy should have arrived on my doorstep like the morning paper, tied with a bow for me to unwrap.

I have some of all three, I want more of all three, but the longer I am Jonathan's mother, the more separate they've become.

I have decided I like *different*. That perfect future doesn't matter so much. The littlest things like looking at Jonathan seated next to me on another silent trip in the car, brings me joy.

Normal isn't as important as it used to be.

A mother once said to me after an emotional sharing of experiences, "God says Jonathan is perfect, right now, the way he is."

I thank God for her willingness to pass that along. She's right. Even with his differences, God made Jonathan perfectly. I will run alongside Jonathan the rest of my life, cheering him to do great things (that's my job), but I don't have to fight 'who' Jonathan is. For me, that's huge.

My hope is in the Lord. My happiness is in the Lord. But what about my idea of normal? Shouldn't that be God's idea, too, and not mine? Today, God sees him as perfect. And for that matter, that's the way God sees my husband, my other children, and me as well.

Life is good when I stop to drink that in.

RESOURCES

When our developmental pediatrician gave us a name for Jonathan's differences, we all breathed a collective sigh of relief. There was a name for it. And then we realized we had no idea what to do about it.

The doctor didn't give me a reading list, phone book or a list of resources. She didn't so much as *tell* me what to do, as point me toward an open doorway. She left most of the discovery to me.

I hope this book has pointed you in the right direction. Again, I am not a doctor, researcher, scientist nor overachiever, thus this limited list of resources.

This list does not mean your child is autistic, has PDD, dyslexia, Aspergers, severe autism, or two left feet. It's to show you what one mother, along with a few hundred others, has read, e-mailed, called or researched. I hope it gets you started.

Resources and Websites

Future Horizons, Inc.
721 West Abram
Arlington, TX 76013
www.FutureHorizons-autsim.com
info@FutureHorizons-autism.com

Cure Autism Now
5455 Wilshire Boulevard, Suite 715
Los Angeles, CA 90036 - 4234
(323) 549-0500
(323) 549-0547 (fax)
info@cureautismnow.org
www.cureautismnow.org

Unlocking Autism
P.O. Box 237
Walker, LA 70785
Telephone: 225-665-7270
www.unlockingautism.org
HOTLINE: 1-866-366-3361

Autism Research Institute (ARI)
4182 Adams Avenue
San Diego, CA 92116
Fax: 619-563-6840
www.autism.com/ari
ARI publishes a quarterly newsletter, *The Autism Research Review International*, which relays current research in the field of autism and related disorders. Also, ARI's website lists doctors who agree with the Defeat Autism Now protocol.

Autism Network for Dietary Intervention (ANDI)
P.O. Box 335
Pennington, NJ 08534-0335
www.AutismNDI.com
e-mail: AutismNDI@aol.com

Developmental Delay Resources
4401 East West Highway, Suite 207
Bethesda, MD 20814
Telephone: 1-800-497-0944

Fax: 301-652-9133
www.devdelay.org
e-mail: devdelay@mindspring.com

www.SI-Challenge.org
for sensory integration information

For testing at 18 months:
php.iupui.edu/~rallen/chat.html

Diet Support:

www.autismndi.com
www.gfcfdiet.com
www.celiac.com
www.nowheat.com/grfx/nomilk/index.htm
www.candida-yeast.com
www.houstonni.com (enzymes)

Books

Special Diets by Lisa Lewis, (Future Horizons, Inc., 1998)

Special Diets, Two by Lisa Lewis, (Future Horizons, Inc., 2001)

Children With Starving Brains, A Medical Treatment Guide for Autism Spectrum Disorder, 2nd Edition, by Jaquelyn McCandless, MD: A doctor's explanation about how it all fits together.

Unraveling the Mystery of Autism and PDD, by Karyn Seroussi (Broadway Books, 2000, 2002): A mother's story and research that led to a cure for her son.

Treating Autism, Parent Stories of Hope and Success, Edited by Stephen M. Edelson, Ph.D. and Bernard Rimland, Ph.D. (Autism Research Institute, 2003): Uplifting, intelligent and hopeful; truthful stories from families all over the U.S. about their struggles and successes in treating their children with autism.

*Includes a voluminous chart with 22,300 parent ratings on the effectiveness of specific drugs, biomedical/non-drug supplements and special diets.
*Includes Autism Treatment Evaluation Checklist (ATEC)

Getting Rid of Ritalin, by Robert W. Hill, Ph.D. and Eduardo Castro, M.D. (Hampton Roads, 2002): How Neurofeedback Can Successfully Treat Attention Deficit Disorder.

A Symphony in the Brain, by Jim Robbins (Grove Press, 2000)
A thorough presentation of the history of brain wave biofeedback, or neurofeedback.

The LCP Solution, by Jacqueline Stordy, Ph.D. and Malcolm J. Nicholl (Ballantine Books, 2000): The Remarkable Nutritional Treatment for ADHD, Dyslexia and Dyspraxia.

The Out-of-Sync Child, by Carol Kranowitz.

Understanding Sensory Integration, Maryann Colby Trott, M.A.
with Marci K. Laurel, M.A., CCC-SLP and Susan L. Windeck, M.S., OTR/L (Therapy Skill Builders, 1993)

Biomedical Assessment Options for Children with Autism and Related Problems:
A Consensus Report of the Defeat Autism Now! (DAN!)
by Jon Pangborn, Ph.D. and Sidney M. Baker, M.D.(2001)
(purchased through Autism Research Institute)

A Guide to Scientific Nutrition and
Guide to Intestinal Health in Autism SpectrumDisorder
Both Authored by Kirkman Labs
Order by contacting www.kirkmanlabs.com

More Books About Autism:
go to: www.futurehorizons-autism.com

About Vaccinations

SafeMinds
Sensible Action for Ending Mercury-Induced
Neurological Disorders
14 Commerce Drive, 3rd Floor
Cranford, NJ 07016
908-276-8032
www.safeminds.org

The National Vaccine Information Center (NVIC)
512 West Maple Ave., Suite 206
Vienna, VA 22180
Telephone: 703-938-DPT3
800-909-SHOT
Fax: 703-938-5768
www.909shot.com
e-mail: info@909shot.com

Testing

The Great Plains Laboratory
9335 West 75th Street
Overland Park, KS 66204
Telephone: 913-341-8949
Fax: 913-341-6207
www.greatplainslaboratory.com
(Order a Peptide Test (digestive problem with gluten
and casein) and/or the OAT test for gut bug/yeast
questions. Tests are free to order, and only cost
when you send them in for processing.)

Doctor's Data
P.O. Box 111
West Chicago, IL 60186
Telephone: 800-323-2784
www.doctorsdata.com

Diet and Non-Drug Supplements

Kirkman Labs
P.O.Box 1009
Wilsonville, OR 97070

Telephone: 503-694-1600 or 800-245-8282
Fax: 503-682-0838
e-mail: sales@kirkmanlanbs.com
A great source for gluten/casein-free vitamins and
supplements, including colostrum (immune booster).
(They publish a free catalogue of their products)

Nordic Naturals - (Essential Fatty Acids)
3040 Valencia Ave., #2
Aptos, CA 95003
Telephone: 831-662-2852
Fax: 831-662-0382
www.nordicnaturals.com

Omega Nutrition (EFA's)
6515 Aldrich Road
Bellingham, WA 98226
Telephone: 800-661-3529

Miss Robens
P.O. Box 1149
Frederick, MD 21702
Telephone: 800-891-0083
www.missroben.com
e-mail: info@missroben.co,m

Gluten-free mixes and products

Gluten Solutions
737 Manhattan Beach Boulevard, Suite B
Manhattan Beach, CA 90266
Telephone: 888-845-8836
www.glutensolutions.com

Kinnikinnick Foods
10306-112 Street
Edmonton, Alberta
Canada T5K 1N1
Telephone: 1-877-503-4466
www.kinnikinnick.com
e-mail: sales@kinnikinnick.com

Allergy Resources
557 Burbank Street, Suite K
Broomfield, CO 80020
Telephone: 303-438-0600

Rexall Showcase International (essential fish oil concentrate)
853 Broken Sound Parkway, NW
Boca Raton, FL 33487-3694
Telephone: 888-22-REXALL
corp.rexall.com

QUESTIONS

1. How early can I expect a diagnosis?

Doctors hesitate to diagnose before age three. However, you can begin helping your child long before that. If you observe differences, ask yourself, if they were to intensify, would it be undesirable? For example, a child talking early is different; however, you want that ability to expand. On the other hand, a child that doesn't seem to mind discomfort—hot, cold, a scratch, etc., is also different. If that were to increase (insensitive to dangerous levels of discomfort) it would not be good. If a three-year-old is reading (good) but never talks (bad) there's a problem. Trust your instincts and do something. Get a diagnosis later.

2. What do I do if I suspect developmental differences?

I would absolutely hold off on any vaccinations (avoid the flu vaccine) until I was certain of my child's immune system/sensitivities, delay them as long as possible, and then insist on only one shot at a time with several weeks passing before getting another. Get a titers test to see if your child has sufficient immunity and does not need a vaccination. Ask to read the label on the vaccine to make sure it does not contain thimerosal (a mercury-like preservative). Test for yeast and gut bugs. Remove gluten and observe any improvement. Remove dairy and observe any improvement.

Based on the differences, apply appropriate therapy. Lack of speech - speech therapy. Lack of responsiveness - applied behavioral therapy (ABA) or sensory integration therapy. Poor language skills, processing disorders, read *Children With Starving Brains*, and begin the appropriate nutritional supplements. They can't hurt, and the sooner you begin the quicker, more complete the chance of recovery.

3. My child has some serious problems. I'm trying to find help, but can't.

Begin with a national organization listed in the Resources section. Even if your child's diagnosis is different, they can often guide you in the right direction. Call the Unlocking Autism hotline.